Praise for 

"*UP!* blends heart and strategy in a way that's rare. It helps women design careers (and lives) that align with who they are—and where they want to go next."

IVY ROSS, chief design officer for consumer devices at Google and *New York Times* bestselling author of *Your Brain on Art*

"Kelly Mooney's expertise in corporate America shines throughout *UP!* Her insights on building authentic professional relationships are particularly valuable for women navigating complex workplace dynamics."

BRET JOHNSEN, chief financial officer of SpaceX

"*UP!* delivers practical career strategies that are spot-on for women to take charge of their careers and lives, without being one-size-fits-all. I wish I had had this book earlier in my career!"

SAORI CASEY, chief financial officer at Sonos and former vice president at Apple

"The unwritten rules of workplace advancement, written down. This is the insider knowledge every woman needs."

DAVID BELL, chairman emeritus of Interpublic Group and member of the Advertising Hall of Fame

"Ambitious and grounded. *UP!* teaches you how to reach the summit, but it also reminds you to enjoy the climb."

SHANNON GLASS, vice president of Global Nike Direct

"Kelly and Katy Mooney have cracked the code of the essential skills needed to advance and thrive on the journey to the C-suite. While written with women in mind, I believe *UP!* would be a valuable read for all college grads on a path to the 'good life.' I highly recommend *UP!*"

MICHAEL CROOKE, former CEO of Patagonia

"Across cultures, I've seen women face the same universal challenges at work—being heard, seen, and supported. *UP!* helps you pause, reflect, and move forward with more clarity and intention. It's thoughtful, practical, and refreshingly real."

LULU RAGHAVAN, president of Asia Pacific at Landor

"*UP!* takes us on a journey of self-discovery and begins in the place many of us take a long time to figure out: how to lead ourselves in charting a career path that aligns with our own values and builds confidence as we progress. I'm pleased to say this is it—the perfect guidebook."

SCOTT KERSLAKE, founder and former CEO of Athleta, strategic advisor and professor

"As a fellow champion of women in the workplace, Kelly brings the perfect balance of pragmatism and optimism to giving professional women the coaching they need and deserve. From the importance of 'finding your fit' (I'm partial to a good dressing room analogy) to 'thinking big(ger),' it's never too early, or too late, to unlock your own possibilities."

MARISA THALBERG, Forbes Hall of Fame chief marketing officer and founder of Executive Moms

"*UP!* is that big sister I wish I'd had. No matter your race, gender, or background, it will help you achieve the career and life you want (and deserve!) for yourself. Read it!"

MALISSIA CLINTON, executive vice president, general counsel at Meritage Homes

"*UP!* is the book every woman with a dream should read. As a CEO, I relate to the highs and lows. Sometimes you feel unstoppable and sometimes like a busted can of biscuits, but *UP!* reminds you that's all part of the journey."

KELLY COOK, CEO of David's Bridal

"When I started Jeni's, I wish I'd had two things: a business advisor and a founder-life coach. Kelly has been both to me—and now she's bringing that wisdom to women everywhere. Wherever you are in your career, *UP!* offers life-changing advice."

JENI BRITTON, founder of Jeni's Splendid Ice Creams and founder/CEO of Floura & Co.

"*UP!* demystifies career growth by showing that small, everyday behaviors create lasting impact."

DR. VIJAY PENDAKUR, leadership and team culture expert and author of *The Alchemy of Talent*

"What I love about *UP!* is how grounded it is in reality. Kelly and Katy acknowledge the messy truth of work and still show you how to move forward with skill and intention."

COCO BROWN, founder and CEO of The Athena Alliance

"As the father of two young professional women, I can't think of a better gift than this playbook to guide them as they traverse their careers . . . and their lives."

MICHAEL BILLS, partner at VENN Growth Collective

"This book is AI—Actual Intelligence—for professional women, written by two exceptional sisters with decades of real-world experience navigating the ups, downs, and roundabouts of work and life. It's the single book every ambitious woman needs."

KATE DELHAGEN, pre-tired Nike exec, angel investor, and board director

"*UP!* is like having an experienced coach by your side: It guides you to go deeper, reflect, uncover hidden beliefs, and expand your possibilities and choices. Then, like a good coach, it moves you into action with practical exercises that help accelerate your transformation."

JEFF TRITT, founder of Onward Growth Partners and former North America talent leader at IBM iX

"A must-read for every woman navigating the modern workplace. This powerful, step-by-step playbook shows you how to tap into your agency, take bold action, and design a career—and life—you truly love."

JODI BRICKER, CEO, board member, and business advisor

"*UP!* offers more than advice; it's filled with actionable steps that will bring clarity and success to YOUR career and life."

JAMIE BARCELONA, vice president of people services at Donatos Pizza

"The workplace is rarely a meritocracy. *UP!* provides the tools to navigate this reality, rise into positions of power and influence, and become the leader who drives the change the world desperately needs."

DOUG ULMAN, vice chair of Pelotonia and former CEO of Livestrong

"You don't have to rely on luck the way I did. Kelly and Katy's *UP!* offers practical guidance and proven tools to accelerate your career growth and take charge of your professional journey."

DIANE KLEIN, former executive vice president and chief financial officer at NBC Universal and MGM Studios

"This is the book I wish my younger self had read right after graduation. It's full of lessons learned the hard way, distilled into one actionable guide."

TROY ACHONG, former executive vice president at Paramount

"My team had the amazing opportunity to work with the Mooney sisters firsthand, and their coaching was truly transformative. Their insights and energy inspired my team to level up in ways they didn't think possible."

MELISSA LEMBERG, vice president of digital transformation at LogicMonitor and former global services leader at Salesforce

"This book captures the hard-won wisdom of what it really takes to build a meaningful, beautiful life. It's equal parts inspiration and instruction, a road map for leading yourself, making courageous choices, and creating the life you long for. It's taken me a lifetime to learn many of these lessons. What a gift this is for anyone at a crossroads, ready to rise into what's next."

LAILA TARRAF, former chief people officer of Allbirds, Peet's Coffee & Tea, and Walmart.com

"Too much talent waits to be seen and valued—only to feel stuck and overlooked. *UP!* is the wisdom we actually need: practical ways to lead yourself, think bigger, and work with confidence and integrity."

SEBASTIAN BUCK, cofounder of Enso

"*UP!* is honest, wise, and full of practical tools that help you turn uncertainty into confidence and forward motion. It's not just a career guide—it's a thoughtful road map for anyone looking to grow, lead, and define success on their own terms."

TESS ROERING, former chief marketing officer at Athleta and CorePower Yoga

"Kelly Mooney masterfully shares insightful experiences with powerful words of wisdom for every woman on the rise. With authenticity and a voice that inspires, she is the perfect person to share this journey. A truly remarkable read!"

SARAH C. BAZEY, founder and former CEO of American Highway

"This book delivers sound, practical advice and strategies for professional women at all stages of their careers. It is a much-needed guide written by women who've personally faced obstacles and succeeded."

BONNIE MARCUS M.Ed., CEC, author, speaker, executive coach, and host of *Badass Women at Any Age* podcast

"I watched Kelly Mooney navigate every challenge this book addresses—from being the only woman in the room to leading as CEO to scaling the business that we ultimately sold to IBM. From my firsthand experience, I can tell you this: *UP!* is not based on theory. It's based on real-life experiences. Too many women wait to be seen and valued, hoping someone will help champion their careers. Kelly and Katy have created a practical, no-nonsense playbook every woman deserves—one that teaches you to lead yourself first. I wish I had *UP!* early in my career. It's awesome!"

NANCY KRAMER, founder of Resource/Ammirati and chief evangelist and senior partner at IBM Consulting

"*UP!* completely nailed it for me. Kelly and Katy break down all the ways women can feel stuck in their careers and turn them into clear, actionable steps toward the success they're capable of. I can't wait to share it with every woman in my circle."

DEBBIE KRISTOFFERSON, former marketing executive at Walmart, Peet's, and Included Health

"Kelly has been an inspiring leader and role model throughout my career. We worked together 20 years ago, and I still draw on those experiences when coaching my teams. This book distills her decades of insight into actionable strategies that help women succeed at work—wisdom I was fortunate to witness firsthand."

SANDRINE KUBINSKI, senior vice president at American Eagle Outfitters

"*UP!* meets women where they are—honest about the realities of work yet optimistic about what's possible. Kelly and Katy Mooney offer clear, practical guidance to help women lead with purpose and create careers on their own terms."

JENNIFER SOMER, CEO of A.L.C. and former president of Dr. Martens

"Both Kelly and Katy Mooney have played key roles in developing me as a leader. Their experience, wisdom, and generosity have benefitted me greatly, and I'm so excited that their new book, *UP!*, will allow so many others to benefit from their wisdom as I have."

ANDI BALDWIN, CEO of Profitable Ideas Exchange

"A refreshing, actionable guide for women ready to step into their power. *UP!* turns career growth into a personal awakening—practical, inspiring, and deeply empowering."

NEELU KAUR, speaker, organizational psychologist, and author of *Be Your Own Cheerleader*

"This is the book that needed to be written, and Kelly and Katy are the perfect duo to do it. They are both seasoned professionals who have seen a little bit of everything in their careers and have generously shared their wisdom through *UP!*. It's a perfect guide for women aspiring to build momentum and meaning in their careers."

JOHN KADLIC, CEO of Parallel Path

"Every woman aspiring to advance her career should read this book—that's the only 'should' you'll find here. What sets it apart is its practical, actionable approach: real examples you can implement immediately. Kelly and Katy deliver grounded, no-nonsense insights that help women maximize their potential at any career stage."

NICKI PARR, CEO of Women's Economic Ventures

"*UP!* zeroes in on and masterfully solves the short shrift that women have lived with for far too long. With this book, women now have proven success strategies to advance their careers from the start, so they no longer have to wonder why they didn't 'get the memo.'"

DEBBIE PHILLIPS, Biden–Harris administration leadership coach and founder of Women on Fire

"Kelly Mooney is the woman other women go to when the moment really matters, including me. She delivers strategies that cut through the noise and kindness that never pulls a punch. What she's put into these pages is what so many of us have been lucky to receive from her in real life: insight, language, and strategy that changes what you do next."

ANGELA SCOTT, founder of The Office of Angela Scott

More Than a Pep Talk

The Playbook for Every Woman on the Rise

FROM THE FOUNDERS OF EQUIPT WOMEN

KELLY MOONEY

with **KATY MOONEY**

www.amplifypublishinggroup.com

UP!: The Playbook for Every Woman on the Rise

Second printing. This Amplify Publishing edition printed in 2026.

For more information, please contact:
Amplify Publishing, an imprint of Amplify Publishing Group
620 Herndon Parkway, Suite 100
Herndon, VA 20170
info@amplifypublishing.com

Library of Congress Control Number: 2026903970

CPSIA Code: PRV0626B

ISBN-13: 979-8-90026-064-8

Printed in the United States

To Gloria Steinem, who, at a small dinner party of women leaders in April 2016, asked, "Why aren't each of you doing more?" That question started everything.

And to all the women who came before us—the pioneers, troublemakers, glass-ceiling breakers, leaders, provocateurs, educators, entrepreneurs, activists, and door-openers—we salute you and proudly stand on your shoulders to lift up the next generation of changemakers.

CONTENTS

PART 3
FIND YOUR FIT

PART 4
THINK BIG(GER)

PART 5
GET IN THE GAME

Foreword

Dear Reader,

When I first saw the title *UP!*, I smiled, because that is exactly where we should all be heading. Up in our careers. Up in our confidence. Up in our impact. But here is the truth: Moving up has never been about waiting for permission. It is not about squeezing into a mold that was never made for us or following someone else's rules. It is about leading with intention, making bold choices, and defining success on our own terms.

That's why I love this book. *UP!* is not about empowerment; it is about what I call INpowerment. I have never liked the word "empowerment" when it is attached to women. We don't talk about men needing to be empowered. Empower suggests someone else hands you the power, as if you did not already have it. But you do. You have had it all along, just like Dorothy and her ruby slippers. She could always go home. She just needed to believe it. The same is true for us: The power is within.

I know this because I have lived it. I have been the only woman in the boardroom. I have felt the pressure to shrink myself to fit in, and I have heard the doubts that come when you are told you are "too much." But I have also seen what happens when you stop apologizing, when you use your voice, and when you surround yourself with people who lift as they climb. That is when real change begins.

Kelly and Katy Mooney know this, too. Together, they have created a playbook that is practical, inspiring, and refreshingly honest. They do not just talk about resilience, confidence, or bold choices; they show you how to practice them. They share stories, tools, and exercises that will help you rise without sacrificing who you are. And because they wrote this as sisters, there is a candor and warmth to these pages that feels like having not one but two trusted mentors in your corner.

As the self-proclaimed Chief Troublemaker, I have built my career on rewriting the rules that were never written with us in mind. I believe women do not just deserve a seat at the table; we should redesign the table entirely. And I know that when we rise together, we create a collective force that accelerates progress for everyone.

This book is that lift. It is a reminder that moving up does not have to be lonely. It can be joyful, purposeful, and fueled by a powerful pack of women supporting one another.

So here is my invitation: Do not just read this book—work with it. Do the exercises, reflect on the questions, and put the strategies into action. You will feel the shift. You will see yourself moving up, your way.

You have got this. You have had it all along. And with Kelly and Katy's guidance, you will find the clarity, confidence, and courage to step into the power that is already yours. That is what I call INpowerment.

SHELLEY ZALIS

Founder and CEO, The Female Quotient

Introduction

I have to be honest. I spent the first half of my career people-pleasing, burning out, and never asking for what I wanted. It didn't have to be that hard.

I grew up with six sisters and two brothers in a small, rural town in Ohio. My sisters and I shared a tiny bathroom where, at any given time, one of us was in the shower, someone else was at the sink brushing her teeth, and one was standing in front of the mirror putting on makeup while the other four were impatiently banging on the door to get in. Perhaps because the girls dramatically outnumbered the boys in our family, it never occurred to me to think of my gender as an advantage or a limitation. My parents focused on rules, curfews, and chores. It all seemed fair to me.

They raised us to be thrifty, obedient, and self-reliant. We shared nearly everything: clothing, bedrooms, and bicycles. They paid for us to attend an in-state, public university and expected us to work each summer. After my first year of college, I was intent on following in my brother's footsteps as the public pool manager. He'd done the job at 19, so I assumed I could do it at that age, too. As it turned out, the local parks and recreation bosses thought otherwise. They decided that the role required two women to do the job that just one man had done three years earlier. The kicker? These two women would have to *split* the salary of $200 per week!

This was the first time I'd been exposed to something so nonsensical—and that I now know was discriminatory and sexist. I didn't know what to do or say in response or how to stand up for myself. I fumed about how unfair it was, but I found a friend to do the job with me and got on with it. I had to—I needed the job.

In the early days of my career, I was eager, earnest, and naive. My first job out of college was a junior position at a highly respected industrial design firm. I didn't realize it then, but I also landed a great boss. He gave me work beyond my skill set, brought me to senior client meetings that I had no business attending given my lack of experience, and gave me candid feedback that helped me grow. He also challenged me to identify my values, an assignment I didn't appreciate at the time but later became a life compass when I needed it most. To my disappointment, two years after I started, he left the firm and moved across the country, leaving me to fend for myself.

The next seven years were rough without a manager to support and champion me. My boss changed so often that I was rarely sure who I was reporting to. My annual reviews were useless because no one had exposure to my work for more than a handful of months. When I started managing people myself, it was with zero training. I was often the first to pull into the parking lot in the morning and one of the last to leave late in the evening. I was expected to work weekends and sometimes holidays to meet client deadlines. I wanted to be a team player, so I said yes to nearly everything, not knowing how this would impact my physical health, personal life, and sense of what was normal in the workplace. And there was nobody I could turn to for guidance.

When my firm was acquired by a global holding company with ambitious plans to expand worldwide, I was excited about the growth opportunities that were bound to present themselves to me. Well, I was excited until I happened to discover that my male colleague was making twice my salary. He was the same age, with the same level of education, in the same role with the same title and the same span of responsibilities. Everything was the same, except that he was earning double what I did!

Admittedly, he had a commanding presence. He was big in stature, walked boldly through the halls, and spoke persuasively to company leaders with a charming British accent. I asked my boss why someone with the same experience and responsibilities as I had was making twice as much money. The answer was shocking: "He's married and has a family to support. You don't."

Whoa. I called my former boss to ask for his advice. He said, "You know what to do. Remember the values we talked about years ago? Use them." He was right. Two of my top values were "respect" and "fairness," both of which were being violated. I was undervalued, underappreciated, and underpaid. How could I continue working there when I wasn't being treated fairly? This was the second time I was shocked by how I was being treated, and once again, I lacked the skills and confidence to do anything about it. But I began to question everything I had previously believed to be just "part of the job," and eventually I realized that I had been letting other people hold the keys to my life. I had been allowing my career to happen *to me*. I wasn't making it happen *for me*.

Without a manager I could turn to for support and advocacy, I had to take matters into my own hands. So I left to join a communications company I'd collaborated with on a project for Apple while working at the design firm. The company's founder was a vibrant woman who recruited me to work for her. She said, "I can see you're really smart. I want to create a new role for you, something you're excited about. C'mon, it'll be fun!" It felt like an invitation I couldn't resist. I wrote my own job description and negotiated a work schedule that gave me time to focus on my health and new marriage. For the first time, I felt like I had some control over my career.

A few years into this job, the founder introduced me to coaching, an experience that began to shift things for me in a substantive way. Suddenly, I was acutely aware of all the ways I hadn't been spending my career currency—my time, effort, and emotional, physical, and intellectual investments in myself. I started to see all the opportunities I'd left on the table along the way. My coach helped me to think more expansively—to broaden my aperture. She helped me to identify and articulate my strengths. She emboldened me to think bigger about what I wanted in the future and how much money I wanted to make. She helped me role-play difficult conversations. She encouraged me to network with people I was curious to know but considered beyond my level. She helped me prioritize what matters most when building a family. She helped me unlock my potential so I could see myself fully and begin to drive my career (and life) with clarity and intention.

Over the next few years, I moved from being an individual contributor to a team leader and then a department leader. When the company announced that it was searching for a president, it didn't occur to me to apply because I assumed I wasn't qualified for such a big role. Numerous men in the office weren't deterred by those same concerns, however, and eagerly applied for the job. Only when a friend asked me, "Why not you?" did I consider this role for myself. Her simple question stopped me in my tracks. *Why not me?* I repeated those words to myself over and over.

I could see that, despite the growth I'd experienced, I was still holding myself back. Waiting to be seen and promoted. Assuming that my contributions would be valued by others. But I was the one who needed to value myself. I was the one who needed to say what I wanted.

And in that moment, a seismic shift happened. I realized I had had the power to shape my career all along. This was thrilling and terrifying. *I can do this job! Wait, can I do this job? Yes, I can absolutely do this job!*

With this new insight, I raced back to the office and told the founder that based on my experience and contributions, I believed I was best equipped for the role and I wanted the opportunity. I think she was proud and relieved when she quipped, "It's about time." She saw my potential but wanted me to see it for myself. For the first time in my life, I did.

Soon thereafter, I was named president, and nine years later, became the company's CEO. During that time, I had two children, became the founder's business partner, wrote two books, gave hundreds of speeches, and was featured in numerous high-profile publications. Together, we brought on private equity, acquired a New York–based business, and, in 2016, sold the combined company to IBM, where I served as its digital consultancy's first chief experience officer in North America. At IBM, I was appointed to a global task force that assessed why so few women were advancing through the ranks, despite being hired at the same rate as men out of college. Today, I serve on the boards of both public and private companies, including their compensation committees, which has given me a close-up perspective on organizational dynamics, leadership pipeline strategies, and evolving talent-related policies.

The big hairy problem that's still a problem

Here's what I see: Most organizations underinvest in you when you're below the middle management level for a few reasons. For one, they're afraid they'll have wasted time and money on you if you leave for something better—even though the top reason professional workers leave a job is lack of career growth and development opportunities (the irony!). Many organizations operate under the assumption that only senior-level leaders require extensive development because they make the high-stakes decisions. Finally, they prefer to invest in capabilities that benefit the entire company (e.g., processes, tools, and technology) rather than invest in you, your growth, and your future.

If your employer isn't looking out for your best interests, who will? There's only one correct answer, and that's *you*. It took nearly 20 years before I truly understood this for myself.

My biggest mistake along the way was allowing my career to unfold in front of me, as if I were sitting on the couch watching it on TV. Out of ignorance or passivity or both, I didn't do a whole lot of stuff that would have made all the difference during those critical early years of my career. Here are some of the things I didn't do:

- I didn't seek out mentors.
- I didn't advocate for myself.
- I didn't think about what I wanted.
- I didn't ask for promotions or a career path.
- I didn't understand why networking mattered.
- I didn't figure out how to navigate office politics.
- I didn't have money conversations, even with friends.
- I didn't learn how or when to negotiate compensation.
- I didn't create boundaries, then worked myself to exhaustion.
- I didn't request training that would have dramatically increased my skills and confidence.

Can you relate?

Hope is not a strategy

For nearly two decades, I was waiting and hoping to be seen, valued, and rewarded. As the saying goes, though, "Hope is not a strategy."

Everything I've experienced over the course of my career—the good, the bad, and the ugly—has contributed to who I am today and to what I have accomplished. I love the life I've built, so I know this is where I'm supposed to say that if I had a chance to do it all again, I wouldn't change a thing. But that's not true. My early career was harder than it needed to be—some of it was downright agonizing! If I had known early on that I could *shape* my own experience by making smarter, more deliberate choices and being more purposeful and proactive, I absolutely would have done that. Would things have turned out differently? Probably. But my journey would have been driven by my own goals and desires, rather than shaped by other people's decisions.

Katy, my sister and the coauthor of this book, has had a very different career from mine. After graduating in the top 10 percent of her law school class, she began her career as an attorney at a major firm, but within a few years, she knew she belonged in a more creative and collaborative field. She went on to become a brand strategist, a marketing executive, a consultant, and an executive coach, working with world-class creative agencies, big-name global companies, and scrappy start-ups.

"For a long time, I didn't think of work in terms of a career, and I never considered how I might advance in any of the roles I had," says Katy. "I always assumed I would get promoted if I outworked everyone else. Wrong! I worked like a dog but had a string of terrible managers, none of whom saw it as their responsibility to support my development and success. I had no idea how to advocate for myself or build relationships with people who would support and champion me. I made a lot of mistakes. So I went from job to job, trying to learn new things and looking for some kind of sign that I had landed in the right place and finally would take root and grow. It just didn't happen that way.

"I worked for lots of different organizations, and none of them felt like a true fit for me, but I consistently developed and honed valuable, transferable skills that ensured I'd always have options. Along the way, I discovered that I had a gift for managing people; helping them understand their skills and strengths and championing their success came naturally to me. Eventually, this led me to the work I do today as a leadership and performance coach and professional development instructor. I traveled a bumpy road to get to this place, but those years of on-the-ground business experience allow me to relate to whatever my clients are going through."

Following our different paths, Katy and I limped through most of our early- and mid-career years without getting any of the straight talk or strategic guidance that we now know would have changed everything for both of us. That's something like 30 career years between the two of us without a map or a compass or any way to figure out the smart moves that would get us somewhere. We never had a playbook, but we really needed one. Ultimately, we were both lucky to end up where we did, but luck isn't a strategy, either!

Realizing that professional women today are not receiving more information or support than we did, Katy and I founded Equipt Women in 2021 to help women when they need it most—when they're establishing or growing their careers. Since then, we've worked with hundreds of women of all ages and career stages from organizations of all types and sizes. We give them the practical tools that allow them to take control of their lives, whether they're just getting started or need a boost midcareer. Over and over, we see their eyes widen as they realize the immense power they have to shape their careers and futures. Every time these transformational moments happen, a raucous high five goes on in our heads.

Careers and lives will follow their own path, or you can direct them. This book focuses on the latter. And while the ability to impact your career trajectory is greatest in your first few jobs, it's never too late. Take control now and steer your career toward where you want it to go—up!

Why you need *UP!* now

After decades of slow, steady progress, momentum for advancing women in the workplace has stalled. Even though women are better educated and more skilled than ever before, they are still hired, paid, and promoted at lower rates than men at every level.

As a professional woman today, you're working within a system that's not designed to support you, and sometimes it's even working against you. The sad truth is that the workplace will never be entirely free of bullies, tribalism, and people who want to hold you back. These barriers can make it feel like a struggle to grow your career—we understand; we've been there! That's why you have to become the CEO of your own life. Learn the smart plays and inside secrets that allow you to lead yourself and take control of your professional fate. That's what *UP!* can do for you.

This playbook is practical, proven, and inclusive

UP! is everything we've learned that we wish we had known early in our careers. The truths, insights, strategies, and hacks in this book will help you go from heads down to heads up and create your life rather than settle for it. *UP!* will fuel more confidence, opportunity, and fulfillment as you take charge of your career. And there'll be no more waiting and hoping for your lucky break. You will *make* your lucky break.

UP! is a playbook with six primary strategies:

1. Lead Yourself
2. Own Your Choices
3. Find Your Fit
4. Think Big(ger)
5. Get in the Game
6. Love Your Life Along the Way

The first five strategies are organized into five parts with dozens of tactics you can apply every day, no matter the role you're in or the organization you work for. They integrate seasoned insight, sensible advice, real-life stories, scripts for difficult conversations, and proven coaching exercises. The sixth strategy, Love Your Life Along the Way, is woven throughout the book because your personal life is happening right now, alongside your work life. These inspirational interludes will help you find joy and fulfillment at any stage of your career and life.

My personal stories are shared at the beginning of each of the five parts of this book. However, the insights and tactics that appear throughout are informed by the experiences and wisdom of countless professionals we've worked with or learned from over the course of our careers.

These rock stars include the following:

- The dozens of business executives and HR leaders at large, medium, and small organizations who helped shape and vet the concepts shared in this book and in Equipt Women programs.
- The recruiters and HR teams we worked with to hire more than 800 people, as well as the various coaches who have guided us along the way.

- The team of MBA students at UCLA's Anderson School of Management who collaborated with us to conduct research as part of the Applied Management Research program.
- The authors and thought leaders whose work has inspired us the most: Julia Boorstin, Brené Brown, Marcus Buckingham, Julia Cameron, James Clear, Carol Dweck, Adam Grant, Sheila Heen, Sally Helgesen, Marshall Goldsmith, Elise Loehnen, Marshall B. Rosenberg, and Douglas Stone.

We've intentionally sought voices that reflect the full spectrum of women's workplace experiences, recognizing that challenges and solutions vary based on individual circumstances and systemic factors. Throughout this book, the term "women" refers to anyone who identifies as a woman or has navigated workplace dynamics from that perspective, including non-binary individuals who share these experiences.

The stories you'll read in the IRL (In Real Life) sidebars are real. They're derived from surveys and conversations with hundreds of women around the world across various industries and career levels. While we've changed names and some details to maintain confidentiality, every story reflects genuine workplace experiences and the strategies that helped these women navigate their careers more effectively.

Don't just read this book—"do" it!

Like any playbook, you can read it from front to back or jump to whatever section relates to what's going on in your life. No matter how you choose to read the book, be sure to do the "Think about it" and "Make a move" exercises at the end of each chapter to integrate what you're learning into your experience. This is how the seeds of real growth and change are planted.

Throughout *UP!*, you'll find mini-scripts for tricky conversations (try these!). The language in the scripts is important, but remember that your tone, delivery, and timing are important, too. Practice these scripts and adapt them to make them your own.

Don't worry about being perfect. The goal is to become a more effective and comfortable communicator.

Treat this book like a workbook. Dog-ear the pages, highlight phrases that ring true for you, and write in the margins. Use the blank pages at the back of the book to capture what you're learning. Make it yours! Return to it throughout your career to help guide you through little moments or big decisions. Use it with the free *UP!* digital toolbox, which is loaded with more resources and templates at equiptwomen.com/upbook. Even better, read this book with a journal nearby to capture important messages and track your progress. Consider reading it with a friend or colleague, or forming a book club.

You will notice the word "should" never appears in our guidance (except in this sentence) because we don't believe there is one way, one path, one approach that works for everyone in every situation. Instead, we use "can," "could," "consider," "may," "might," "try," and other words and phrases intended to help you step out of your comfort zone as you explore what works for you.

You will also notice bits of wisdom linking one part of the book to the next, reminding you of the importance of enjoying your life along the way.

Don't try to do everything at once. Instead, take it in small doses so you learn the strategies and develop new habits and skills at your own pace. If you notice you're resisting something you encounter in the book, it might be a clue that it's something you need to work on. (Just sayin'.)

Reading—and then doing—this book will cultivate what I call career wellness: building a successful, fulfilling career alongside a personal life you love. You'll gain confidence, open up new opportunities, and create greater financial security. More joy and less drudgery—because work doesn't have to suck! You will feel equipped to take charge of your career, so you aren't waiting and hoping for a lucky break. You will *make* your lucky break.

If you're new to the work world, *UP!* will give you a robust foundation. If you're stuck in your career, *UP!* will give you the jump start you need to get moving again. And if you're on a roll, *UP!* will help you keep the momentum going and prepare you for bigger opportunities ahead. This is *your* playbook. Make it work for you.

It's your life—take charge of it

UP! challenges the outdated notion of "having it all" and invites a different way of thinking: What matters most is having what matters to you. With that clarity, your way forward isn't about climbing the same old ladder to the top. It's about recognizing the power within you to take charge and move toward your goals–on your own terms, from any direction.

> Up is progress.
> Up is proactivity.
> Up is purpose.
> Up is a state of being and becoming.
> Up is the realization of bigger and better possibilities.

There are many ways to feel up, get up, stand up, ramp up, level up, rise up, and stay up.

Up is *up* to you.

Part 1

LEAD YOURSELF

FESS UP REST UP S
UP SKILL UP POWER
POWER UP STAND U
UP RAMP UP GEAR U
P PUMP UP 'FESS UP
UP OPEN UP RISE U
P STEP UP LIFT UP
MOVE UP FIRE UP S
SHOW UP LEVEL UP
ST SPEAK UP MOVE
'FESS UP REST UP S
UP SKILL UP POWER
POWER UP STAND U

Where do you want to go?

That's an easy question to answer when you're heading out to do errands or taking a road trip. When it comes to your career or your life, it's not so easy.

Here's another tough one: Who do you want to become?

When you were a kid, well-meaning adults were always asking you what you wanted to be when you grew up. This probably got you thinking about jobs you might be good at or careers that could be fun, which in turn may have led you to your major in college or even to the job you have today.

So here you are. By now you've realized that these questions aren't settled once you've completed your education or found a profession that seems to suit you. (If you haven't reached that point yet, these questions might feel even more overwhelming.) You may also have realized that arriving at one of these destinations is just the beginning of learning where you want to go and who you want to be. Then it hits you that this will be an ongoing journey—a forever journey, really—and you think, *Ugghhh, how will I know what to do next?*

Some people find it thrilling to head out on an adventure without an itinerary. To others, it's scary—even paralyzing—to contemplate even the shortest outing with no road map to guide them. For your lifelong journey, here's a little secret: You actually have the world's best GPS—you. Only you can lead yourself in the direction you want to go.

When you lead yourself, you don't leave what happens next to chance. You take responsibility for who you are and what you do and work to become the best version of you. When you lead yourself, you develop your self-knowledge and take intentional steps to move closer to your goals and the life you want to live. This inner development will bring definition and specificity to your understanding of what you care about, what you're capable of, and who you are from the inside out. As your self-knowledge increases, your vision for your future becomes clearer and you get stronger.

A standing yoga pose requires the lower part of your body to be solidly planted on the ground while your upper body reaches outward. Without a solid foundation beneath you, you'll struggle to hold the pose. Without extending yourself fully on top, you won't gain the benefits of the pose. When both your upper and lower body are engaged, you can realize the full potential of the pose.

Similarly, leading yourself provides a firm grounding in who you are today while making space for you to stretch and evolve into who you will become tomorrow. When you lead yourself, you feel less anxiety and worry. Life feels more doable. Lighter. Less intimidating. More exciting. Decisions are easier to make. You become super clear about what feels right for *you,* which opportunities and relationships to pursue, and what (or who) to avoid.

When I was in my 20s, I didn't know there was something I could be doing to lead myself. I had the mindset of many young professionals I knew at the time: Graduate. Get a job. Work hard. Play hard. Sleep little. And do it all over again day after day, weekend after weekend.

This led to patterns of destructive behaviors. Working too many hours. Partying too much. Showing no sense of self-responsibility or safety. I hitchhiked home from bars while drunk. I dated guys who didn't respect me. I hung out with friends who made even worse decisions than I did, which helped to ensure that my standards stayed exceptionally low.

On the job, however, I was killing it. I was doing excellent work and getting great reviews from my boss. Because I was performing at a high level, I assumed everything was good. Besides, I was young!

One Saturday, I went to a neighborhood bar to watch the Ohio State football game with friends. Feeling generous after receiving a small bonus, I bought beer for the whole gang. This lasted for hours until I ran out of money. When the game ended, everyone left, including the skanky guy I mistakenly thought I was dating. (Given the quickie sex we'd just had in the musty stairwell, my judgment was seriously lacking on many levels.) It was dark, late, and cold. I was broke and buzzed and couldn't find anyone to give me a lift home (no Ubers then). I was an effing mess.

The pay phone ate my last quarter when I called one of my sisters for a ride and got her voicemail instead (no cell phones then either). Just at that moment, a hunched, disheveled old man who had been sitting on a bench nearby shuffled over to me. I was looking around anxiously to see if I knew anyone nearby when he reached into the pocket of his threadbare coat and pulled out a handful of change. In a raspy voice, he suggested I take enough for bus fare—a quarter and a dime—and told me which bus to catch. My face hot with shame, I thanked him and took his money. I cried all the way home.

Looking in the mirror later, I wondered, *Is this who I am? Is this what I want out of my life? Hell no!* I shouted back at myself.

As I had done on so many earlier occasions, I could have blamed my friends or the guy who deserted me that day. But this time, I saw my icky situation for what it really was: a painfully clear sign that I wasn't driving my own life. I was thrashing around, leaving everything to chance or to my own poor judgment. I suddenly understood that I had to take responsibility for myself—my attitude, my choices, my behavior. And I realized that it was time—right then and there—to start making some decisions about where I wanted my life to go.

You don't have to hit rock bottom like I did to come to the conclusion that you want your life to go somewhere better. You may be languishing in a dead-end job or a relationship that's unsatisfying. Or you could just be stuck in routines or habits that are holding you in place. But when you finally have the little lightning bolt moment I did (or maybe yours will be a less dramatic, persistent nudge), you'll know you're ready to lead yourself.

It's a great feeling when you realize how much power you have to influence your future. There are smart things you can do today—starting right now—to become more sure of who you are, what you believe, and what you're capable of. Together, these acts of self-leadership will give you the confidence, strength, and agility to go where you want to go and be the person you want to be as you move through every chapter of your life.

When you lead yourself, you will pay more attention to every aspect of your life. You will react less and make more thoughtful, intentional choices. You will know what's important to you *and* what you need to get where you want to go. Self-leadership puts *you* in the driver's seat of your life, which is exactly where you want to be.

So go on, take the wheel. Giddy*up*!

1

Stand for something

Know what defines you.

Your personal values are an expression of what's most important to you in your work and life. They are ideals that are true to you, and you appreciate seeing them in others. They often determine how you spend your time, how you behave, and how you respond to what's happening around you. They influence every practical aspect of your life, from where you live and work to who your friends are to what you do with your money. As much weight as they hold, though, most people aren't fully conscious of their values. Unless specifically asked to consider how they would describe their values, they likely don't give them much thought. Which is a shame, given what a tremendous asset your values can be in building the future you hope for.

In fact, your values are the foundation of self-leadership. On a good day, they help keep you grounded, grateful, and focused. On a day when you're struggling, they remind you of who you are and what you care about and help get you back on track. On any kind of day, your values help move you toward your goals—but first you have to know what they are!

Start by reviewing this list of possible values. Scan it for a few minutes and select five to ten words that resonate with you. Resist thinking about what other people would expect you to choose. All that matters is that your values speak to what's important to you. If the words on this list don't capture your values, choose your own.

Accountability	Creativity	Growth	Power
Achievement	Courage	Health	Purpose
Advancement	Equality	Impact	Recognition
Adventure	Excellence	Independence	Responsibility
Authenticity	Fairness	Integrity	Security
Balance	Fame	Leadership	Self-respect
Beauty	Family	Learning	Stability
Belonging	Freedom	Loyalty	Spirituality
Community	Friendship	Love	Wealth
Compassion	Generosity	Optimism	Wisdom

Define each word for yourself. Words mean different things to different people, so define what they mean to you. If "health" is a value for you, it could mean that you place a high priority on physical fitness, such as working out and eating well. Or that same value could mean holistic health that incorporates the physical, mental, emotional, social, and spiritual aspects of your well-being.

Look again at your values and definitions. Do they ring equally true to you, or are some values much more important to you than others? Do any of them overlap? If so, you might consolidate words and refine your definition to reflect the value's essential meaning to you. For example, if "generosity" and "community" are values you've identified, could "impact" be a term that accurately encompasses both? Try to narrow your list to the five values that are most important to you. (Why five? Because you want to keep your values front of mind, and most people find it difficult to remember more than five things at once.)

Identify key behaviors associated with each value. These behaviors should relate to how you live each value or how you aspire to live them. For example, the behaviors described below might relate to someone's "health" value. If health is one of your values, your list of behaviors could be very different. Only you can say which behaviors make a value real for you.

- Following physical and mental health news
- Scheduling routine wellness appointments
- Exercising regularly
- Following a particular diet
- Sleeping eight hours each night
- Limiting alcohol consumption
- Disconnecting from work emails and texts when at home
- Socializing with friends and family
- Managing workload and boundaries

This exercise will take some time. Don't rush it or give up. Let the five values you land on simmer in the back of your mind for a week or two. Then return to it and refine or finalize your list of values, definitions, and behaviors. Keep it handy so you can refer to it as you contemplate new challenges or circumstances. And refresh your list as your sense of self and priorities evolve over time. What mattered most to you as a college grad may be different from what matters to you at a later stage of your life.

Use your values. Now that you have a vocabulary for your values, use your values to guide your actions and advocate for your wants and needs. For example, if you value flexibility but have been experiencing burnout, you could have a conversation with your manager that goes something like this:

> *"I'd like to talk about the number of days I spend in the office and the possibility of reducing it from three to two days. Being on-site on Tuesdays and Thursdays when my key meetings occur would allow me to make the most of my in-person time in the office and continue contributing at a high level. Could we try this for three months and see how it's working for the company, our team, and me?"*

Or if recognition is an important value to you and you want to find a way to experience it more at work, you could make this suggestion to a coworker:

> *"I place a lot of value on being recognized and appreciated for my contributions. I know that many of our team members feel the same way. What do you think about implementing an informal peer recognition system? It could be as simple as calling out small wins in our weekly team meeting. I think the boost of acknowledgment would be motivating to people and inspire them to continue delivering great work."*

IRL

Allie was in a funk, but she wasn't sure why. Feeling burned out, she had recently taken a low-stress, entry-level sales job, despite having 10 years of experience with tech start-ups and an advanced degree. While the job was more manageable, she found she just didn't care about the work. It didn't provide a sense of purpose.

She reflected on her values, such as "community," "connection," "learning," and "impact," which had driven her decision to get a degree in nonprofit management. She also reflected on her career journey, hoping to recall prior roles where she had felt her values were most engaged. The job that immediately came to mind was when she was a counselor at a summer camp during her college years. She enjoyed developing relationships with the kids that deepened over the course of the summer. And she loved teaching them and watching them grow.

And then it clicked: That experience felt fulfilling because it was rooted in her core values, something that was missing from her current job.

Once she understood why her easy sales job had not remedied her career burnout, she sought out (and landed!) a different job in the company that focused on learning and development. In this role, she was able to work with people who were eager to grow and build skills to advance in the organization. This job was challenging and immensely gratifying. Reconnecting with her values helped her make her way to exactly where she wanted to be.

When you feel out of sorts about your work, or your path is uncertain, your values will remind you of what's important. Let them be an inner compass that guides you when you need it most. Let them help you recognize when it's time to make a change in your career. Or give you confidence and conviction on a shaky day. Or know whether something is worth fighting for or not. Let them help you find friends, colleagues, and mentors who care about what you do. Let them help you lead yourself.

Think about it

What is your single most important value right now? Why is it so important to you?

Identify one new behavior that could strengthen how you live this value.

2

Practice empowering habits

Develop the discipline you need to do big things.

The word "habit" probably makes you think of things you routinely do. Grabbing your morning coffee. Flipping through the photos on your phone. Singing to yourself in the shower.

But habits are more than just actions. They are tiny scripts inside your brain that integrate your thoughts, emotions, and actions. They become the patterns that govern how you think, feel, and behave. These are powerful patterns that have an outsized influence over the quality of every aspect of your life. They impact your health, relationships, and finances, as well as your upward mobility, well-being, and productivity.

We generally categorize habits as good or bad. Good ones are beneficial or virtuous: You floss your teeth. You write thank-you notes. You turn off the light when you leave a room. Bad ones are detrimental or inconsiderate: You stay up too late. You interrupt when someone else is speaking. You leave dirty dishes in the sink for someone else to deal with. Habits can also be conscious behaviors that you choose (flossing) or unconscious behaviors you're unaware of (interrupting).

Instead of thinking of habits as good or bad, consider them in terms of whether they are *empowering* or *disempowering*. Empowering habits make you stronger and move you closer to your goals, while disempowering habits undermine you and prevent you from reaching your goals.

Empowering habits give to you. They support you and what you want for yourself. They expand your capabilities, create more opportunities, generate energy and motivation, build self-assurance, and prompt more growth and learning. They lift you up.

Your empowering habits increase your confidence and help you feel in control of your life. They might include journaling, exercising regularly, expressing gratitude, weekly planning, healthy eating, or continuous learning.

Disempowering habits take from you. They drain your energy, erode your self-esteem, limit potential opportunities, and steal time from your most supportive relationships. They drag you down.

Your disempowering habits stunt your personal growth and inhibit your success in achieving your goals. These habits could include negative self-talk, stress eating, gossiping, avoiding difficult conversations, or procrastination.

Science shows that repeated behaviors strengthen neural pathways, making habits more automatic over time. So why don't you just cultivate more empowering habits and eliminate your disempowering habits? Because disempowering habits are easier and more convenient. They feel good in the moment. And empowering habits take time and effort and occasionally some pain to develop—you have to go out of your way to build them. Sugary donuts or a nutritious breakfast? The empowering choice is obvious, although it's not always easy. But it's likely to become an easier choice if you're more intentional.

Being intentional means planning ahead so you don't have to rely on willpower in the moment. Rather than approaching this as a big makeover of your habits, break it down into these small, separate steps. Over time, this will gradually shift the balance of empowering versus disempowering habits in your favor.

Become aware. Take a week or so to simply notice your habits. Look at your morning routine, how you behave in meetings, how you engage with friends, and how you unwind. Pay particular attention to habits that are supporting you or undermining you. Note a handful of these kinds of habits to observe more closely.

Observe your habits. Notice the impact of these habits on your physical health, mental well-being, relationships, and productivity. Are they aligned with your values? Are you dedicating time to your empowering habits? Are they giving you a demonstrable boost? Are there times of day, places, situations, or people present when your disempowering habits occur? Is stress, boredom, fear, or something else a trigger?

Categorize your habits. Once you've noticed your habits and how they make you feel, sort them into two categories: empowering and disempowering. If a habit is supporting your goals, creating new possibilities, and lifting you up, it's an empowering habit. You want more of these. If a habit is preventing you from achieving your goals and keeping you down, it's a disempowering habit. You want fewer of these.

Replace old with new. Use a common healthy eating strategy—add in to crowd out—to make way for a new empowering habit. For example, instead of immediately engaging with your phone when you wake up, use the first 10 minutes of your morning to stretch or take a walk around your neighborhood. Try this for 30 days and assess the changes you notice.

Bundle. Attach a new habit to something you already do or like to do. For example, combine a five-minute meditation with your morning cup of tea. Or if you want to start walking more, reward yourself by listening to your favorite podcast at the same time.

Zero in. To ensure that the positive change you're making sticks, add or subtract just one habit at a time. After you've established the new behavior (about 30 days), turn your attention to the next habit you'd like to develop. If you try to take on more than that at once, it's less likely the change will last.

IRL

After a full day in the office, Rianna spent most nights sprawled on the couch scrolling on social media. She looked forward to it as a welcome relief from the pressures of her job and the stresses of her personal life. Hours passed, and though she often felt like she had wasted the evening, she was unmotivated to do anything else.

When her roommate urged her to give social media a break, Rianna acknowledged the daily habit might be contributing to her problems, not alleviating them. So she vowed to put her phone in another room after dinner for one week and read for 30 minutes instead. After one week, the half hour turned into an hour and became a new habit that she relished. She felt less tense and more optimistic.

Soon after, Saturdays became a day for discovering new books at used bookstores, a treasure hunt to eagerly anticipate. Seeing how her outlook had been improved by her new habit, Rianna removed TikTok from her phone and now just checks it from time to time on her laptop.

As you develop new empowering habits and leave old disempowering habits behind, you move closer to the fully capable person you aspire to be. Practicing empowering habits is a hugely impactful act of self-leadership. They are an intentional investment in your future self—a critical bridge you build to get from where you are to where you want to go.

Think about it

What is one disempowering habit you want to eliminate? What is one empowering habit you want to create or develop further?

Make a move

Establish a new empowering habit that replaces a disempowering habit. Practice this new habit for 30 days, then evaluate how it has impacted you.

3

Experiment a lot

Courage is cultivated.

Like most children, when you were young, you probably climbed trees to dangerous heights, threw yourself off the high dive at the pool with reckless abandon, or rode your bike fearlessly pretending to be in the X Games. At about the age of 10, though, things probably began to change for you.

Research shows that girls become more cautious about taking physical and social risks at that age. They start to be influenced by cultural norms and expectations they have begun to notice and by social conditioning they experience at home, in school, or through the media.

All this is exacerbated by the feedback patterns girls receive to be "good" or "careful." They are seldom encouraged to "shake it off" or "get up and try again" the way boys routinely are. By the time they're adults, many have become averse to taking risks, which may have a profound, long-term impact on confident decision-making, career trajectory, and earning potential. Unacceptable!

The antidote to this crippling cautiousness is to cultivate courage through experimentation.

Incorporating small experiments into the regular rhythms of your life puts courage to work for you—no lab coat or goggles required. When you approach life as a series of experiments, you challenge yourself constantly. Each experiment deepens your knowledge of yourself—how you think or respond in this circumstance or that, what works for you and what doesn't. As you grow more sure of yourself, you'll become more adept at dealing with uncertainty and adapting to new situations. Then one day, you'll realize you feel gutsy and brave, and jump at the chance to take a big job or move to a new city.

How can you live your life as a series of ongoing experiments?

Shift your perspective. Your aim is not to get an A, to be perfect, first, or a winner. It's simply to grow your courage through experimenting.

Focus on trying. Try new things, things that are unfamiliar to you, even a little uncomfortable. This can span all areas of your career and life, from testing new skills or roles to exploring new foods, travel destinations, or relationships. To make it more fun, team up with a friend. Never mind the outcome, just think about the experience you'll accumulate along the way.

Start with low stakes. Think of an experiment where you might be 10 percent out of your comfort zone. For example, to get better at public speaking, begin talking to strangers in the coffee line and watch what happens. Remember that most experiments can be abandoned, reversed, or quickly modified, so if you're feeling tentative, consider these questions:

- What is the worst possible outcome?
- Can I recover from it?
- What's the cost of not trying?
- Is there a smaller thing to do that I could try first?

Raise the stakes. Think about an experiment that takes you 50 percent out of your comfort zone. For example, to further improve your public speaking skills, volunteer to lead one of your organization's employee resource groups or a project that allows you to facilitate small group meetings of peers. Notice what you're learning about yourself. Maybe you're quick on your feet in a way you hadn't known before. Or you discover you have difficulty projecting in a large room, so you want to strengthen your voice.

Take the stakes higher. Find an experiment where you are 90 percent uncomfortable. Maybe you ask for the opportunity to present to senior leaders at a department meeting. Having practiced in situations with less pressure, you're now better equipped to face a riskier situation. You might feel scared, but do it anyway. That's when your courage grows exponentially.

Make room for failing. Not every experiment is going to feel pleasant or have a successful outcome. But every experiment will teach you something, especially the ones where you flop a little (or a lot). Say you stumble in your presentation to your bosses. The feedback you receive may bum you out for a minute, but it may also be the most valuable insight you gain at this stage of your career. Just process what you've learned, and move on to the next experiment.

IRL

Amaya was an A student her entire life. With clear expectations, a straightforward syllabus, and a predictable grading scale, she excelled. Meritocracy made sense to her: Go to class, do the work, and get a good grade. She had the confidence and skills to succeed.

But she struggled mightily after college when she got her first job working for a venture capital company, where there were no obvious rules for success. She kept her insecurities and frustrations to herself because she felt embarrassed by her inability to navigate this new domain. She remained quiet in meetings, not wanting to offer a wrong answer. She observed her male peers, who seemed confident in this professional habitat and, as a result, were being assigned more complex projects. On the verge of tears, Amaya confessed to her manager that she didn't know what she needed to do to succeed in her work.

Her manager assured her that she had solid skills and great potential but noted that she seemed to be holding herself back. As the only woman on the team, Amaya had a unique perspective but wasn't sharing it in group discussions. She spent untold hours perfecting documents but hesitated to make time to take on bigger assignments. She was risk-averse in an organization where taking risks was necessary and expected.

Suddenly she realized she would have to take steps that made her uneasy, like asking more questions and volunteering to take on tasks she'd never done before. She started sharing her work while it was still in progress. Although she found herself in unfamiliar territory more than ever before, she could see that she was becoming a valued contributor on her team.

Every experiment you undertake grows your courage to do the challenging, risky things that will expand your universe of opportunity. You will become more comfortable being uncomfortable. You will become more sure of yourself in the face of uncertainty. Most of all, you'll learn to trust your ability to lead yourself no matter where your journey takes you.

Think about it

What's an area of your life where you feel cautious or risk-averse?

Make a move

Do one experiment weekly to become more courageous in that particular area. Note what you are learning about yourself, especially when you fail, or if your experiment turns out differently than you expected.

4

Activate your strengths

Build muscles by doing what pumps you up.

Part of moving up is doing work that makes you feel *up*.

Early in your career, you're exposed to various people, situations, functions, and tasks that help you develop valued skills. As you become good at things, you establish your reputation, you're given more responsibility, and colleagues want to work with you.

These are incredible upsides, but just being good at something isn't enough and doesn't automatically lead to job satisfaction. A better strategy is to become good at something you like doing. This is what makes it a *strength* rather than just a skill: being good at it, enjoying it, and feeling energized when doing it.

According to Marcus Buckingham's work, a strength is an activity that strengthens you, and a weakness is an activity that weakens you—even if you're good at it. That last part is mind-blowing for most people, but it makes sense when you think about it. A lack of enjoyment or energy for what you're doing makes you feel weak, not strong. All on its own, being good at something is not a strength.

Begin tuning in to your strengths by thinking about how you feel before, during, and after an activity. For example, are you excited and energized when you begin your day because you'll be doing something you enjoy? Are there particular tasks or meetings you look forward to? Do you lose track of time when you do the task or attend the meeting? Do you feel fulfilled at the end of the day? If you're experiencing any of this, your strengths are likely in play at work, so kudos to you!

If you're not feeling any of that, you may have become good at something that's not enjoyable or energizing to you. You don't mind the accolades and being perceived as a valuable teammate, but you dislike the work itself. You may have always disliked it or have grown to dislike it. Maybe you notice yourself procrastinating or hoping someone else jumps in to do it.

What gives?

When you're good at something at work, your manager and teammates assume you like it. Then what happens? You end up with more and more of this same work. When you're not crazy about this work, eventually it becomes tedious and exhausting. Dissatisfying. That's a big clue to ask yourself whether this thing you're good at is a strength or just a competency. If you do it well but you don't enjoy it or it drains you, it's not a strength.

This distinction between a competency and a strength is crucial as you navigate your career and life. Many people fall into a common trap of being good at something they don't enjoy and never uncover their strengths or apply them to the fullest. According to the CliftonStrengths, which has polled millions of professionals, just 17 percent say they employ their strengths "most of the time in a typical day."

However, research shows that when employees can use their strengths in their work, they're more engaged, more creative, and happier. They learn faster, too.

Of course, it's not realistic to expect to feel happy and fulfilled all the time. Every role has mundane activities that must be done on any given day or week (that's why they call it "work"). Early in your career, though, a good goal to shoot for is spending half of your time doing work where your strengths are being applied. As your career advances, ideally, you spend most of your day using your strengths.

To get to that ideal time/strengths ratio, you have to have a clear understanding of what your strengths are! Here's how to pin down that essential intel:

Track your energy. Keep track of how you feel about what you're doing at work over a two-week period. Note the activities that make you feel engaged, excited, or energized in the "I'm pumped!" column. Enter the activities that make you feel disengaged, drained, or bored in the "I'm drained!" column. Whether you track this on your phone or in a journal, it's best to log your observations in the moment or shortly thereafter.

What if you're neither pumped nor drained by an activity—you're just indifferent? Notice that. But the main goal is to identify which parts of your work energize you and which don't.

I'm pumped!	I'm drained!

Do the math. At the end of two weeks, the activities in the "I'm pumped" column are good indicators of where your strengths lie. Try to spend more time doing more of these things. Activities in the "I'm drained" column are indicators of your weaknesses and where you want to minimize your time, if possible. If "I'm drained" activities are a big part of your day, it's important to pay attention to that. Your role might not be utilizing your strengths, and that could be why you don't like your job.

Get more specific. Now consider the factors that contribute to your enjoyment of the "I'm pumped" activities you've identified. These factors might be:

- Whether you are working independently or on a team
- The people you're working with
- The size or type of team
- The subject matter of the activity
- Whether you are strategizing or executing
- Whether you are leading or following

For example, you may have logged "solving complex problems" in your "I'm pumped" column. That's a great start. Now, what else is important to you in relation to solving complex problems? Identify other details that factor into your enjoyment of this work—perhaps the people, the type of project, or the role you're playing.

These details may lead to very different conversations—and opportunities—that relate to your strengths. For instance, you might love solving complex problems in the areas of climate change and housing as part of a cross-functional team working in sprints. Or maybe you love working autonomously to help organizations find greater efficiencies and grow their business. Or perhaps solving complex problems for you involves creating innovative design solutions for a start-up launching a new product.

When you can identify your strengths and talk about them with specificity, it's easier for your manager (and others) to help you find opportunities to apply them more often. It also allows you to demonstrate the value of your strengths to the organization.

What if you really like an aspect of your work, but you're not good at it yet?

If you're motivated to improve, you might have a strength in development. For example, suppose you were asked to give a mini demo to your team about how to use AI tools for market research. You felt nervous because you'd never given a presentation before, but you discovered that you enjoyed sharing your knowledge and facilitating the Q&A with the team. It activated something within you that signaled a potential strength you may want to develop further. It might take years to get good at it, but the journey will likely be gratifying.

Do strengths ever change?

Sometimes. Just like people, strengths can evolve and change. The activities you're jazzed about at work today might not feel the same in five years. Maybe you'll be exposed to new challenges that point you toward different skills and passions. Maybe you'll want to grow in different ways. New strengths can emerge, and old strengths can fade, so keep paying attention to the enjoyment and energy you feel about your work. They are a terrific gauge of your strengths.

Determining your strengths is something only you can do. Other people may notice qualities or skills that you don't recognize in yourself or you take for granted, but they won't know how much (or little) energy and enjoyment you feel inside. Trust yourself and your assessment of your strengths. This awareness will enable you to seek out and advocate yourself for work that activates your strengths, which is rewarding and positions you to be in demand. And it's a win for your employer because when you apply your strengths at work, you will be more engaged and impactful.

IRL

Kathleen had a marketing degree and a few years of experience when she joined a consulting firm as a project manager, the only open position at the time. She excelled in the role, consistently nailed timelines, ensured high-quality deliverables, and met project budget requirements. She routinely received kudos from teammates and leadership. However, despite being good at it, she found her work tedious and uninteresting, and she went home each day feeling drained from organizing spreadsheets and coordinating countless details.

Despite her competency as a project manager, she didn't enjoy what she was doing. She was a big thinker and problem-solver and wanted to do work that utilized her education and previous work experience. Whenever she had the opportunity to collaborate with strategy or market research teams, she showed she had good instincts and always provided valuable insights. Those meetings and conversations were exciting. Although she lacked specific experience in these areas, she loved how it felt to contribute more than just her project management expertise.

Kathleen approached her manager to discuss moving into another role on the team that focused on strategy and tapped into her experience in marketing. Kathleen's manager was supportive because she'd been a consistently high performer, and the organization wanted to keep her. Kathleen knew there would be a learning curve in a new role but was eager to make a lateral move from a project manager to a strategy manager. Soon after, she transitioned to this role and quickly learned the company's proprietary processes and frameworks.

Energized by the strategic thinking and creative problem-solving she was doing in her new job, she later became a sought-after strategist by top clients.

Exercising your strengths turns work into something you actually look forward to. When most of your day is spent doing things you enjoy and that energize you, work no longer feels like work. Part of self-leadership involves paying attention to what makes you feel alive and then pursuing it. Being aware of how you feel will help you recognize when something is right for you. Trust yourself and steer your time and career toward those things. When you activate your strengths, you don't just get by—you thrive.

Think about it

What are your top five strengths? How much of your day is spent applying them in your work?

Make a move

Discuss one of your strengths with your manager, HR leader, or someone who champions you. Ask them to help you find opportunities to use it more often.

5

Speak up

Your voice counts. Use it.

Have you ever watched someone walk into a room and just own the conversation? Their voice is clear and strong, and they appear confident. They have observations to share, ideas to contribute, and questions to ask. When they speak up, others listen—whether it's in a group discussion or a one-on-one exchange. For these people, speaking up feels natural. For the rest of us, it's a learned skill.

If you're outgoing or experienced, finding your moment to speak up in a group setting may seem like no big deal. However, speaking up may be trickier for you if you:

- Are the youngest person in the room
- Are introverted
- Are new to the team or organization
- Are a person of color or the only woman
- Are less experienced than others

- Have a different area of expertise than others
- Have a perspective that diverges from the group

Any of these factors and potentially others may inhibit you from speaking up. In the long run, speaking up matters because it establishes you as a valued contributor and builds your confidence. It matters in real time because if you don't speak up, people may draw unfair or inaccurate conclusions about you.

Don't let that happen.

No matter your age or role experience level, you have something important to contribute to the conversation. You have something unique and valuable to share—your lived experience, observations, ideas, and questions. The world needs to hear from you. Your team needs to hear from you. Your organization hired you to make an impact, not to sit quietly in the corner.

The purpose of speaking up at work is to add value. When you speak up, you may be raising points that others haven't yet considered. You may have insights that could help save time or money or avoid costly mistakes. Your contribution could improve a decision or solve a problem. Your speaking up also helps your colleagues and friends understand and appreciate your unique perspective and your expertise.

There are many moments that require speaking up, but meetings are a good place to start using your voice. Give these tactics a try:

Heads up. Review the agenda in advance if you can. Identify two to three areas where you have something to contribute. Then notify the meeting leader beforehand that you are interested in participating in a particular part of the meeting. This will make them aware and more likely to ask for your thoughts. It will also help you show up ready to engage.

Speak early. When you hear your own voice early on in a discussion, it immediately reduces the pressure or anxiety you may have felt in anticipation of the meeting. When you wait until the end to speak, you could lose your moment if the agenda is cut short or people get antsy for the meeting to wrap up.

Build. Ask questions to expand the conversation. "*Can you elaborate on that?*" is a simple way to engage. Then you might add to their response with "*That's interesting. I'd like to expand on that . . .* " And if your point of view differs from theirs, you might say, "*I've had a different experience*" or "*I'd like to share another perspective on that issue.*"

Keep their attention. Speak clearly and concisely. Make eye contact with members of the group (including senior leaders), whether you're speaking or listening. Be mindful of your body language (e.g., don't slouch, fidget, or fold your arms across your chest).

Be solution oriented. Focus on accomplishing the group's goal. Instead of simply disagreeing with or criticizing another person's position, turn the conversation toward an alternative idea. "*To address our objective of X, I'd like to suggest we explore Y.*" Don't feel obligated to speak up if you don't have something constructive to add. There are already too many people in the world who talk a lot and contribute nothing. No need to be one of them!

IRL

Leah, 27, is a client manager for a global branding agency. Her colleagues are primarily men over 50 who have worked for the company or in her industry for decades. They usually dominate the internal team meetings and client presentations and interrupt her frequently when she's leading a conversation. She feels exasperated and discouraged to the point that she's considering quitting her job.

A fellow teammate observed her frustration and tendency to withdraw and remain quiet when she was talked over. He encouraged her to try a couple of tactics that helped him find his voice when he was in a junior position. At his urging, her first bold move was to meet individually with one of her most vocal, domineering colleagues and say, "I want to grow my skills as a meeting facilitator, and I could use your support and coaching. You might not be aware that it's difficult for other members of the group to speak up with so many strong voices in the room. Do you have any advice on how we stay on track in meetings and hear everyone's point of view, including mine?"

Initially, her colleague was taken aback. He wasn't aware of the dynamic she described, but Leah's constructive approach persuaded him to be part of the solution. Tuned in to his own behavior, he was more careful to let her lead the meeting agenda and solicited her point of view during discussions, which signaled to other teammates to follow his lead.

You can't expect other people to recognize your value if they don't know what's on your mind. You have to take responsibility for making your voice heard, even when it feels uncomfortable. Every time you speak up in a meeting or conversation, you're not just expressing yourself; you're leading yourself—you're demonstrating that you belong in the room and at the table. There will be pivotal moments in your future—in life and at work—where speaking up is a moral imperative. Developing the skill and confidence to speak your mind will serve you now and in the future.

Think about it

When have you stayed quiet at work or in a relationship where you had something important to say? What prevented you from speaking up?

Make a move

Practice speaking up. Pick a low-stakes meeting where you have something to contribute. Ask a trusted coworker to give you feedback on what went well and how you might do even better in the future.

6

Bounce back

*Sh*t happens. Roll with it.*

It's inevitable: Tough things happen at work that are unexpected or unwanted. Organizations merge, restructure, impose layoffs, delay or cancel projects, deny promotions, and enact hiring and spending freezes.

Tough stuff happens in life, too—breakups, rejection, arguments with friends, the loss of someone we love, health or financial challenges.

Any of these events is likely to be upsetting. Or worse, they might cause you to feel paralyzed, anxious, or depressed. But clinging to your fear or disappointment and dwelling on bad experiences are like stepping in quicksand—you're not going anywhere. This is why the ability to bounce back from misfortune or mistakes and power through setbacks is a key skill in every part of your life. Resilience allows you to recover more quickly and not lose your momentum. It also helps reduce stress and allows you to better cope in the face of any kind of change.

Employers value resilient employees because they contribute to a more stable and productive work environment and improve morale. Your resilience benefits you because you can pivot quickly and increase your impact in difficult situations.

Being resilient is a major asset. But becoming a resilient person is easier said than done. Disappointments, anxiety, and personal failures have a way of taking hold of you. How can you get good at bouncing back faster?

Process your emotions. When you experience an event that causes you to feel angry, discouraged, or just plain bummed out, notice your emotions. Give yourself an hour to acknowledge all of your feelings. If something has truly knocked you off balance, take 24 hours, a few days, or even a week if needed to think it through.

Reframe. Now turn your attention from the negative to the positive. What possibilities or lessons have come out of this event? This is known as reframing the situation. Ask yourself a series of questions to flip the script from negative to positive:

- *Did I do my best? If yes, great! If not, what can I improve?*
- *What can I learn from this experience?*
- *What new skills did I discover or strengthen?*
- *What skills did I discover that need to be strengthened?*
- *What unexpected positive outcomes might come from this?*
- *Will this matter in five months or five years?*

Put the learning to work for you. Think about how you will use what you learned to bounce back in the future:

- *How might I apply what I've learned to a future project?*
- *What could I do to help my teammates bounce back from a future setback?*
- *What resources would help me to navigate this effectively?*
- *What different choices would I make next time?*

As you consider these questions, your perspective will shift, and you will discover a constructive path forward. You will also find that you grow through what you go through. With practice, you will bounce back more quickly and instinctively each time you experience a setback.

IRL

Mei spent three months working long hours to build the system requirements for a major website overhaul for a client. After endless rounds of meetings, user research, and approvals, the specifications were submitted. However, the next day, the client canceled the project after deciding to go in another direction.

It turns out that Mei was unaware that the client had also assigned an internal team to work on a different solution. The work Mei and her team had been contracted to deliver would not be used. She was devastated and angry. Why was she asked to conduct the project at all if the work wasn't going to be utilized?

She left the office and went for a brisk walk. Later, she called a former colleague who pointed out all the upsides of what happened: She had produced excellent work, got the experience of doing it, solved a complex problem, and the client paid for the work. Her friend helped her see many positive outcomes from doing the work, even if the company didn't use it. The client's decision to go a different route was not a reflection on the quality of Mei's team's work. The client was probably managing risk and had multiple work streams in motion. Mei wasn't aware of their internal rationale, so she needed to accept their decision and rally her team so they could move on in a positive frame of mind.

She gathered her team and shared the news, thanking them for their individual and collective contributions. Then she asked each team member to share something new they had learned on the project and something they would carry forward to their next project.

Mei's own show of resilience helped her team bounce back and be ready to do it again in the future.

Things that don't go the way you hoped deserve your attention. While your confidence might be temporarily shaken, just give yourself a chance to understand what happened and how it might impact what you do next time around. Then move on. Over a lifetime, there will be days when resilience feels like the most valuable asset you've got.

Think about it 

Recall a recent setback that you found difficult to recover from. What issues or obstacles hindered your progress?

Make a move 

Reframe the setback to focus on what you learned. Note one specific thing you'll do differently in the future because of what you learned.

7

Build your network

It's your lifeline to the future.

Your network is your net worth—the stronger your professional relationships, the more doors open to opportunities that directly increase your earning potential.

Building your network may be time-consuming, and when you're busy with your actual work, it could be hard to find the time to invest in networking. It may also be challenging in a virtual world where most of your workday is spent in front of screens. And for some people, networking feels uncomfortable, inauthentic, and occasionally cringey.

If any of those reasons have prevented you from networking, you're missing out on valuable relationships that can lead to more clients or customers and future career opportunities. Did you know that up to 80 percent of roles are filled as a result of personal and professional connections? Or that 70 percent or more of job opportunities are not advertised online? These jobs are usually posted internally or explicitly created for candidates who recruiters meet through—you guessed it—networking. In short, networking pays.

It's time to build *your* network with high-quality connections. Here's how to get going:

Get live. Remote working and limited business travel schedules don't give you much of a chance to network in person. But there's something about that human interaction you can't get with video meetings or on the phone. So get out there in the face-to-face world. Check out your organization's meetups, join local professional groups or coworking spaces, and attend events on topics that interest you.

See the opportunity. When you think of networking as a chance to meet interesting people, everything changes. Instead of dreading a forced conversation, be genuinely curious about them. You'll feel yourself relax and enjoy a real conversation between one human being and another.

Jump-start conversations by asking about things you're naturally interested in, whether it's the latest technology, a new hobby, or industry trends. Just get them talking about themselves. This takes the pressure off you to be the most interesting person and allows you simply to be interested. Use open-ended questions such as, "*What's something you've been working on that you're excited about?*" or "*What's your favorite app these days?*" Listen intently to find out what they care about, what you can learn, and how they might need your help. You'll find that when you stop trying so hard to network, it's easier to forge a connection.

Be generous. The most powerful networkers aren't the ones hoarding contacts and looking to get something out of every interaction. They're the people who are genuinely interested in supporting and uplifting others. They view networking as building relationships with interesting people, not conducting transactions. Whether you're sharing your expertise, recommending a relevant resource, or opening doors through your own connections, a spirit of generosity goes a long way in building lasting, meaningful relationships that will be there for you down the road.

Make it a habit. Networking isn't a one-and-done proposition; it requires consistency. Dedicate at least one hour each week to networking. Be active on LinkedIn, post on your organization's intranet, and reach out to people in your network. Track your interactions with people in your network to remember the highlights and any actions you planned to take.

Once you've made a great connection, don't let it fade. Send a quick note afterward, and mention something specific you discussed that you found interesting. Check in at least a couple of times per year with a friendly *"How's it going?"* or send a relevant article or comment on their social media posts. This shows you're still engaged and interested in them. Those little touchpoints may turn a onetime chat into a lasting professional bond.

It's important to build connections proactively when things are going great, rather than reactively when things aren't so great. (Dig a well before you're thirsty!) This makes it easier to make a request or ask for a favor when you really need one, and everyone needs one from time to time.

IRL

Lynzie had been heads down as a senior purchasing manager at an apparel retail company for over six years. She enjoyed her work and knew she had a positive impact in her role and on her small team. Yet she heard rumblings in the hallway about a potential company sale, or worse, bankruptcy, that would bring about many changes at the company. This meant her job was probably at risk. Being the major breadwinner in her family and with an infant to care for, she started to panic.

As she tried to gather her resources to hunt for a new job, she realized her network of professional relationships was skimpy. She hadn't spent much time maintaining them since she took her job. Now she had few people to turn to for help.

She summoned the courage to call a former boss and share her situation, asking for guidance. After listening for ten minutes or so, it was clear Lynzie had unintentionally stopped networking and needed to intentionally restart. Her boss talked to her about where to begin without appearing desperate but also reminded Lynzie that it might take time for her efforts to bear fruit.

Lynzie began by updating her LinkedIn profile and connecting with former colleagues, classmates, and professors. She organized coffee and lunch meetings to get reacquainted, ask what they loved about their job, and share her interest in exploring what was next. She asked professional friends for introductions to people in similar roles and to keep an eye out for open roles. She said, "Is there anything I can do to help you?" to show her genuine appreciation and willingness to bring value to the relationships. Through these exchanges, she learned that the most useful question to ask at the close of a conversation is, "Is there someone else you recommend I speak with?" Lynzie secured the names of two recruiters so she could connect with them directly.

It took a few months of concerted effort, but Lynzie was able to jump-start her network, which led to interviews at multiple companies. Even when she learned her job would be terminated, she felt confident and buoyed by the opportunities from her rekindled relationships.

Don't wait for a career crisis to start building your network—start now, when the pressure is low and the possibilities are wide open. Strong relationships don't happen overnight; they grow through ongoing effort. Connections you make today may grow into your next big break, collaboration, or lifelong mentor. After all, networking isn't just about who you know—it's about how you lead yourself toward the opportunities ahead.

Think about it 

How would your feelings about networking change if you approached it as a way to meet interesting people?

Identify five former classmates or colleagues you've lost touch with and restart the relationship. Focus on what you can do for them rather than what they can do for you.

8

Bank on yourself

You will always be your best investment.

How much have you invested in your own future? Maybe you have a savings account or an IRA, participate in a 401(k) plan, or invest in the stock market, digital currencies, or real estate. As you build a career and a life, you may do some or all of those things. But there are other kinds of investments to make in yourself that pay big dividends.

Many professionals overlook the most obvious and beneficial investment they could make—the investment in *themselves.* When you invest in yourself, you're choosing to spend time and money to grow your skills, increase your options, and secure your financial independence. This allows you to make bold moves without being held back by worry or fear. It signifies a commitment to realizing your potential and ensuring you're not leaving any opportunities on the table.

It's time and money well spent. According to Gallup, workers who participate in upskilling programs see an average annual income increase of 8.6 percent. And

39 percent of workers reported they advanced at their current job after completing skill development courses. For some professionals in knowledge-based industries, certifications and licenses may boost weekly pay by 30 percent or more.

Consider these ways you might invest in yourself:

- Grow technical skills and knowledge
- Develop stronger communication skills
- Participate in leadership training
- Earn industry-specific certifications
- Pursue an advanced degree
- Build your network
- Strengthen personal and professional relationships
- Join professional membership organizations
- Cultivate your personal brand and reputation
- Start a side hustle or a business

To create your own investment plan, start by asking yourself:

Where's the growth?

Always invest in something that's growing or emerging with promising signs of growth. To maximize your investment in yourself, identify high-demand skills in your industry or an industry that interests you. Look into jobs and fields that are growing and have high-salary potential, long-term skill relevance, and transferability (how the skill can be easily applied to a variety of roles or industries).

For example, you may decide to develop skills in AI because the market is hot and expected to grow exponentially, salary potential is high, and long-term relevance is strong. Also, AI skills are not limited to tech—they apply to a wide range of fields including health care, retail, finance, legal, education, customer service, operations, and marketing. In contrast, you may avoid learning an outdated software platform, manual skills that will become automated, or certifications that lack industry recognition.

What big problem(s) do you want to solve?

Think about the problems you find intrinsically motivating to solve. There are many challenges the world needs help with: climate resilience technologies, global disease prevention, affordable housing and health care, equitable access to education, renewable energy, food security, and AI ethics—to name just a few big ones.

You may be motivated to solve problems that serve your local community, such as developing mental health resources or reducing food waste. Brainstorm problems you'd be thrilled to be thinking about and collaborating to solve.

What strengths can you apply?

Think about your strengths—what you enjoy doing, find energizing, and look forward to working on. You may be good at these now, or you're on your way to becoming good at them. You'll learn faster and enjoy your work more when you're using your strengths, which are good indicators that you will stick with your development efforts. Also, applying your strengths is more likely to get you noticed, promoted, and rewarded—leading to exponential returns rather than incremental gains.

What's your Sweet Spot Investment?

Now, look for the sweet spot in the overlap in your answers to these three questions. That's the ideal investment for you.

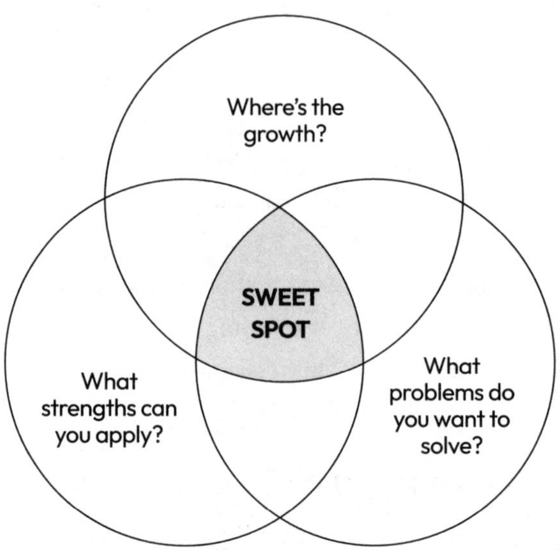

Most employers provide some internal professional development opportunities or offer a stipend for you to pursue outside programs. If you are unsure, ask your manager in a conversation like this:

> *"I'm interested in growing my project management skills and want to take an eight-week online course offered through the local university. This will not interfere with my current responsibilities, and it will allow me to gain a foundational understanding of project planning, risk management, and budgeting. The course cost is $1,595, and I'm confident that I can immediately apply the learnings to our team projects, making it a strong return on the investment. Would you approve this professional development expense?"*

Even if your employer doesn't cover the cost of professional development opportunities, there are loads of low-cost or free options available to you. Build time into your schedule—even 15 minutes a day will make a difference—to dig into resources such as LinkedIn Learning, ChatGPT, YouTube, podcasts, and the public library.

IRL

Dalia was a talent recruiter who excelled at using her network and LinkedIn to find designers and copywriters to work for her creative agency. She loved interacting with the talent and getting to know them in the interview process. She realized, however, that once an offer was extended and accepted, she was always disappointed to have to hand off the new hire to internal teams for onboarding and professional development. She wanted to stay connected to these new employees and help them grow in their roles.

She decided to expand her skill set and pursue certification as a performance coach. This would allow her to tap into her strengths and address her desire to have deeper, longer-term relationships rather than short-lived, transactional relationships. Over two years, she earned her coaching certification, logging on for training several evenings per week and on weekends. It was taxing, but the curriculum inspired her, and she knew she was building skills that would give her more options with her employer and put her in a better position for future opportunities.

After completing the program, she was quickly promoted to a director-level position focused on talent development that came with a higher salary.

Investing in yourself is the ultimate act of self-leadership because you're choosing to bet on your own potential. Much like a financial investment, the compounding effect of investing in yourself over a career is critical because each new skill or certification increases your market value. And no economic downturn or organizational change can take the value of those investments away from you. When you're willing to invest time and money in your personal and professional development, you are securing your future no matter how it unfolds.

When did you last invest in yourself? What motivated you to do so?

Take action on one investment you can make in yourself now that will lead to more opportunity and financial independence in the future.

PART 1 WRAP UP

Self-leadership is your ability to guide your own growth and decisions rather than drifting through life hoping things work out. When you lead yourself effectively, you become intentional about your career path, relationships, and personal development. You make strategic choices that align with your goals and values to create the life you want to live. Self-leadership also makes you incredibly valuable to others—whether as an employee, colleague, or friend—because people trust and respect someone who demonstrates they can manage themselves well. In an increasingly unpredictable world, your ability to lead yourself becomes your most reliable source of stability and competitive advantage.

- **Stand for something** to guide your decisions and behaviors in a way that aligns with what's most important to you.
- **Practice empowering habits** to feel more confident and in control of your life.
- **Experiment a lot** to cultivate courage and overcome fear and perfectionism.

- **Activate your strengths** to be happier and create a greater impact.
- **Speak up** to have your point of view valued and your opportunities expanded.
- **Bounce back** to use learnings from setbacks to prepare you for future challenges.
- **Build your network** to cultivate relationships that advance your career.
- **Bank on yourself** to secure your future.

Take care

Think of your body as your home—the place you live every single day. It's capable of giving you comfort, energy, and joy, but only when you give it the care it needs. This practice of self-care requires purposely tending to all aspects of you to preserve and improve your well-being and happiness.

Here's the thing—self-care requires that you put yourself first, which may be hard for some women to get comfortable doing. Yet it's essential to living your life fully and being equipped to manage the stress that comes when tough stuff happens. In many ways, self-care is self-preservation.

Here's what that can look like.

Show yourself some love. A healthy self-care practice supports your physical, emotional, social, and spiritual needs. That may sound like a lot, but self-care might be small, simple things like drinking plenty of water, chilling with friends, or having an afternoon nap. It doesn't have to be expensive or time-consuming either; it just needs to support you. While a deluxe spa day might be a welcome treat, a 15-minute soak in a hot bath at home might do the trick, too. Think of it holistically; what your head, heart, and body need are interrelated. When you take a break from your devices, for example, every part of you benefits.

Make your own recipe. There's no singular formula for self-care. The activities you choose to engage in will address your unique needs, which might change from day to day or vary over the course of your lifetime. The important thing is to bake self-care into your way of life. Don't wait for burnout, illness, or another kind of wake-up call to show yourself the care you need. Block time on your calendar for social outings, workouts, and phone calls to catch up with long-distance family or friends. Be mindful of nurturing yourself for a few moments to begin and end each day. Use idle time in traffic or standing in line for deep breathing instead of checking DMs. Get lots of good sleep (and don't worry about being a party pooper).

When you take care, you create a lighter, brighter, and more enjoyable "home" for yourself.

Part 2

OWN YOUR CHOICES

'FESS UP REST UP S
UP SKILL UP POWER
POWER UP STAND U
UP RAMP UP GEAR U
P PUMP UP 'FESS UP
UP OPEN UP RISE U
P STEP UP LIFT UP
MOVE UP FIRE UP S
SHOW UP LEVEL UP
ST SPEAK UP MOVE
'FESS UP REST UP S
UP SKILL UP POWER
POWER UP STAND U

Too many women are passive participants in their own careers and wonder why things aren't turning out how they hoped.

Why? There are many contributing factors, from societal conditioning to family dynamics to structural and systemic bias. All of these are real. But you have choices.

The truth is that you are the boss of your life. You are not at the mercy of anyone or anything unless you choose to be. Your choices determine the most important things that happen to you. When you don't own your choices, you blame your upbringing, society, employer, partner, or family. You let the years pass, wallowing in resentment and regret. However, when you own those choices, you will discover your agency, self-confidence, and overall fulfillment in both work and life.

Your life is a series of choices. Some are big, and some are small. Some are meaningless, and others are consequential. Whether you're dead-ass broke, stuck in a job that's going nowhere, or sick of your social life, you have choices. It might not feel as if you do, but you do. *That's* an eye-opening truth.

> You can choose to struggle.
> You can choose to figure it out on your own.
> You can choose to ask for help.
>
> You can choose to get more education.
> You can choose to keep doing what you're doing.
> You can choose to explore a new career opportunity.
>
> You can choose to scroll for hours on social media.
> You can choose to limit your time on social media.
> You can choose to delete your accounts.

You can choose to believe that money will just work itself out.
You can choose to let someone else handle your finances.
You can choose to become financially savvy.

You can choose to develop new skills.
You can choose to stick with what you know.
You can choose to become an expert.

You can choose to wait and hope to be recognized for your work.
You can choose to be resentful when overlooked for a promotion.
You can choose to ask for more money or a bigger title.

You can choose to actively pursue advancement at work.
You can choose to keep your head down, work hard, and hope for the best.
You can choose to strike out on your own.

You can choose a consistent workout regimen.
You can choose to work out when you have time.
You can choose to avoid working out at all.

You can choose to pursue maximum earning potential.
You can choose to be financially secure.
You can choose to deprioritize compensation.

You can choose to eat a healthy diet.
You can choose to snack throughout the day.
You can choose to eat whatever you want whenever you want.

You can choose to use a dating app to meet people.
You can choose to date people you meet in real life.
You can choose not to date at all.

You can choose your friends.
You can choose to take breaks from friends.
You can choose to end friendships that aren't working for you.

You can choose to marry.
You can choose to be in a committed relationship.
You can choose to be single.

You can choose to start a family.
You can choose to delay starting a family.
You can choose friends as family.

You can choose to go to that party.
You can choose to go to that party for an hour.
You can choose to skip that party.

You can choose to stay up late.
You can choose to go to bed early.
You can choose what your body needs.

Choices aren't easy. Or binary. And often, not free. Instead, many take time, money, planning, and trade-offs. Patience and sacrifice. Losses and gains. Self-doubt and self-assurance. Trial and error (lots of errors).

The average adult makes about 35,000 decisions a day. Most of those decisions are unconscious, such as remembering birthdays or instinctively smoothing over conflicts at work or with friends. But plenty of them feel consequential. *Do I take that new job? Do I move for this career opportunity? Do I take time off for family?* No wonder some people become overwhelmed by the agony of choice—all those anxiety-ridden "what ifs?" that swirl around in their heads.

What if I make a terrible choice?
What if I regret my choice?
What if there is a better choice?

This worrisome mental merry-go-round often leads to indecision. Yet avoiding making a choice is also a choice. In fact, not choosing is maybe the worst kind of choice you can make. It means you're letting someone else make the choice for you or allowing fate to determine what happens to you.

When you recognize that nearly everything in front of you—your attitude, your behavior, your relationships—is a choice, you begin to understand just how much of your life is in your control. That powerful realization will cause you to see opportunities instead of obstacles. Owning those choices means taking responsibility for making the decisions that will impact your life and for maximizing the outcomes of those decisions. When you own your choices, your life expands in exceptional ways:

Your gratitude deepens.
Your relationships strengthen.
You understand yourself better.
You sleep more soundly.
You have more impact.
Your income grows.
You become the CEO of your life.

When you own your choices, your life will not be perfect. In fact, it will always be imperfect. But it will be 100 percent uniquely yours.

By my mid-20s, I'd been a bridesmaid 11 times, and every close friend of mine had married. They teased me for being a late bloomer or waiting for the ideal man. Fortunately, I was self-aware enough to know that I was not yet ready to choose my life partner, as I was still exploring who I wanted to become, my political views, career ambitions, and personal dreams. I broke off a couple of long-term relationships because I felt confined and misunderstood. How could I choose that?

After a two-year dating hiatus, I met someone through a friend. He was the first person who looked into my eyes when I spoke instead of looking around the room for someone better. My career in design inspired him to pursue a more creative profession. He supported my ambition to get promoted and have more responsibility at work. I knew within 30 days of dating that we would be together for life. I didn't wait to be chosen; I chose him. And yes, he chose me, too. But to underscore that this was my choice, I asked him to get married. It was not the bent-knee type of proposal. It was a deep, heartfelt conversation that I initiated. We were on the same page for what we wanted in life. We had aligned values. We were partners in the truest sense of the word. We skipped the engagement ring and sealed the deal with matching wedding bands that we chose together.

Sometimes you'll make choices that don't work out as you'd hoped. That's okay because you will make new choices based on your learning that will continue to move your career and life forward. And you'll learn that there are no "right" choices, only choices that are right for you now.

When you don't own your choices, your fate is in someone else's hands. Own them, and you have the power to shape your life.

The choice is *up* to you.

9

Control what you can control

You're the boss of you.

Life has a way of throwing curveballs when you least expect them. Maybe your organization is restructuring . . . again. Perhaps your partner made a major decision without consulting you. Maybe one of your parents received a scary diagnosis. Or the news cycle is sending you spiraling.

It's easy to get swept up in the drama of what's happening around you and worry excessively about what might happen next. That's not only exhausting and unproductive—it can be debilitating. But here's what changes everything: recognizing that while you can't control what happens to you, you have complete power over how you respond to it. You can control what you think, say, and do. You can choose how you respond to the world around you.

Recognizing what's outside your control reduces anxiety because you intentionally stop wasting mental energy on it. Similarly, knowing what you can influence also helps you manage anxiety. The idea of distinguishing between what you can and can't control dates back centuries to Stoicism. In the late 1980s, Stephen Covey introduced the Circles of Influence framework to show people how to direct their energy more effectively. Here's a simplified breakdown and how it works in practice:

You have 100 percent control. No one else gets a vote here—this is your complete domain. You are entirely able to make it happen or change it. For example:

- What you think, say, or do
- Your priorities and goals
- Your boundaries

You have some control. You can nudge, guide, or influence these things, but other people or factors also have an impact on them. For example:

- What others think, say, or do
- Your relationships
- Organizational culture
- Your future
- Your health
- Your community

You have zero control. You can't change these things, no matter how much you worry about them. For example:

- The past
- Accidents
- Weather
- Pandemics

There's a common thread among all three categories—how you respond. While worry, blame, or resistance might be your first reaction to what's happening, none of these things will give you control. The healthiest response is intentionally redirecting your time and energy to what you can control and influence. For example, when someone behaves in a way that is disagreeable, you don't have to respond with more of the same. Instead, you can calmly choose to disengage or lower the temperature by saying any number of things, such as:

> *"This conversation feels charged. Let's take a break and talk about it tomorrow."*
>
> *"Thank you for sharing your perspective. We seem to have a different point of view on this."*
>
> *"I don't appreciate the tone of this conversation. Let's talk when you're ready to discuss this calmly."*

Notice how the dynamic changes when you exercise control over your response. How can you develop more control of your own words and actions?

Listen to understand. Practice active listening from a place of understanding, not defending or complaining. Ask clarifying questions and summarize what you heard. You might not agree with what you're hearing, but you'll hear it more fully, which will better inform your response. Take your time and think before you speak. An immediate response is often not as thoughtful as it could be. Quietly count to 10 before responding. Or take 10 minutes or even a couple of days to give yourself time to think through what you want to say. There's power in a pause.

Flip the script. Consider how you'd feel if what you're about to say was said to you. By trying to understand their position, you can choose to strengthen a relationship through your response rather than weaken it. Would your words (and tone) make you feel heard, respected, or supported? If not, reshape your message to be positive or civil.

Assume good intentions. Most people are well intentioned and aren't trying to upset or hurt you. They may care about their relationship with you and might be receptive to whatever reasonable thing you have to say. Be aware that your immediate reactions are often driven by emotions that stem from a place of fear, so resist reacting in the moment. Stay calm and composed. If necessary, take a break to get a handle on your emotions. Things always look different 24 hours later.

Tune in to your body language. Your physical demeanor may send signals you don't intend. A furrowed brow may indicate you disbelieve someone when you may just be processing the information. Crossed arms and legs may suggest you're not open to the conversation when you just need a sweater.

Say something. If you have something important to say or contribute, let your voice be heard. Be assertive but respectful. For example, if you disagree with someone, you might say, "*Thanks for sharing your take. I had a different experience that I'd like to share with you.*" Or if you're part of a group discussion routinely dominated by the same voices, you could try:

> *"I'd like Rochelle to finish her thought."*
>
> *"I want to make sure I understand Myra's idea before we build on it."*
>
> *"To ensure we have a broad perspective on this issue, let's include Samantha and Chevonne in the briefing."*

Think ahead. What do you want from this, and how do you want to feel about it in the future? Then work backward: What thoughts, words, and actions are needed from you to create your desired outcome? When you pause to consider your long-term intentions—how you want to feel and what you want to achieve—you can respond purposefully rather than react reflexively. Your words, tone, and presence will become tools for building trust, not tension.

IRL

Nerisha was an analyst at a leading biotech company. At her midyear performance review, she got a "below expectations" rating from her manager, who told her she just wasn't cutting it. This was brutal feedback, all the more so because Nerisha had long been frustrated by a lack of support from her manager. She moped for a while but knew the feedback was true. She could remain resentful and lose her job or take in the feedback and use it to improve herself. So she made a plan to spend the next six months focused on just what she could control—her own attitude and actions—one day, one meeting, one conversation at a time.

She showed up every day determined to do her best. She developed relationships with people who could help her improve her work. She planned and led more effective meetings. She strengthened personal connections with her team. It was liberating to just keep her eye squarely on what was in front of her—each meeting, each assignment—and not think about what might happen after six months.

Without her manager doing a single thing to support her improvement, Nerisha received an "above expectations" rating and a full bonus at her annual performance review.

The next time you feel overwhelmed by circumstances beyond your control, choose to control what you can control—your thoughts, words, and actions. Then the power will be in your own hands, allowing you to be the author of your own experience. Use this power to be the person you want to be. The choice is always yours.

Think about it

Think of a time you were frustrated by something you couldn't control at work. Now consider this instance in terms of what you know you could have controlled. How might you have handled it differently?

Make a move

Do one thing each day to practice controlling one aspect of your life that you genuinely have control over. For example, if you want to improve how you interact with other people, practice one or more of the following:

- Use positive, constructive words when speaking to someone you disagree with.
- Listen carefully and wait at least five seconds before responding.
- Empathize with the person you're talking to before sharing your point of view.

Try this for a week and note any impact on your anxiety level or how you feel in general. Continue practicing in other areas of your life where you want to respond to whatever's happening more effectively.

10

Manage your mindset

Curiosity is your secret weapon.

Your boss doesn't respond to your email for two days. What happens next?

Maybe you think, *She's swamped. She'll get back to me when she can.* Or *She's avoiding me because my ideas are terrible.* Or maybe you spiral: *She's not responding because she's planning to fire me!* Same situation, three completely different reactions.

This is your mindset at work. It's how you think about things—the beliefs and assumptions that shape how you see the world and what you believe is possible. It's what your mind is "set" on—whether you see obstacles or opportunities. Whether you assume good intentions or expect the worst. Your mindset influences how you behave, including how you treat others (and how they treat you). That's why managing your mindset is critical to owning every choice you make.

When you're stressed or on autopilot, your mindset often defaults to binary thinking: right or wrong, all or nothing, threat or safety. But you have more control over this mental framework than you might realize. The key question isn't whether your mindset is "right" or "wrong"—it's whether it's helping or hurting you. Is your mindset:

- Moving you forward or keeping you stuck?
- Building your confidence or undermining it?
- Enabling you to be the best version of yourself or something less?

How do you recognize when any of these situations occur, and how can you manage your mindset in that moment?

This is where most people go wrong. Managing your mindset isn't about fighting your thoughts or pretending negative thoughts don't exist. It's not about forcing positive thinking either; you can't muscle your way through it. It's about investigating your thoughts using curiosity as your secret weapon.

Curiosity is effective when you're in the thick of it because it is the antidote to being fixated. It loosens your grip on a specific way of seeing things. This openness can reveal what you might have missed. It also creates space for other possibilities and perspectives. Here's how to use curiosity to manage yours:

How are you talking to yourself? When something's bothering you at work or in your personal life, check in with your inner self-talk. What are you telling yourself about what happened? For example, if you gave a presentation at work that you felt wasn't well received, and you're distressed, what are you saying to yourself about that? Common, unhelpful self-talk might be *I always mess things up, People don't take me seriously,* or *I'm not good at this kind of thing.*

What is your "evidence"? Ask yourself, *Is your self-talk true, or is it just familiar?* Get curious about all the facts. For example:

- How do you know the presentation wasn't well received?
- What feedback did you receive specifically?
- Was the entire presentation not well received, or just part of it?

What else might be true? Consider what else might be true without jumping to conclusions. For example, maybe your presentation could have been organized more effectively. Or it's possible that some people arrived late and missed the setup at the beginning. Or maybe your manager is tough on everyone. Or maybe you didn't give your best effort, and it showed.

Do you need more information? If you're unsure about some details, seek out additional information. For instance, regarding the presentation, you could tell your manager you're eager to improve your presentation skills and would value constructive feedback on your content and delivery. You might ask a colleague who attended the presentation to identify one or two things you did well and one or two areas for improvement next time. By gathering more information, you may discover that you failed to convey some key messages, which could be shared in a follow-up email to meeting attendees. Alternatively, you may find out that you need to rehearse more for the next presentation. On the other hand, you could also learn that your presentation was well received after all!

Practice self-compassion. It's not always easy to cut yourself a break, so try comforting yourself as you would a close friend. You might say to yourself, *Everyone has off days. This doesn't define my abilities.* Or *I'm learning and growing, and that's what I'm meant to be doing.*

Choose a new mindset. Adopt a mindset that helps you. Replace negative thoughts (obstacle mindset) with positive ones (opportunity mindset) that support your growth and learning. For example:

Obstacle mindset	Opportunity mindset
I'm not good at this.	*I'm not good at this yet.*
I always mess up.	*This didn't go as planned, and I can learn from it.*
People don't take me seriously.	*I can improve my presentation skills.*
I have to give a presentation.	*I get to increase my visibility.*

Even with your best effort, some days you will struggle to manage your mindset. Your thoughts are too loud, too fast, and too convincing. This is normal. This is human. On those tough days, try to understand what you need in that moment. Sometimes the answer is rest. Sometimes it's help from a friend, mentor, or therapist. Sometimes it's just acknowledging that today is hard but tomorrow might be different. That acknowledgment alone may be enough.

IRL

When the start-up Elena worked for was restructured, she found herself reporting to Jake, someone who'd joined the company six months after her. The story she immediately told herself was that they promoted him to manager because he's a man and that she'd never advance in this male-dominated company.

This self-talk consumed her. She perceived Jake's feedback as patronizing and viewed new assignments as mere busywork rather than opportunities. Her resentment intensified daily, impacting her work and her relationships with colleagues.

After months of frustration, Elena's mentor asked an uncomfortable question: "What if gender isn't the whole story? What else might explain the promotion?" Elena got curious about her assumptions. As she thought more about it, she realized Jake had five years of client management experience that she lacked. He'd also built relationships across departments while she'd focused solely on perfecting her technical skills.

Elena realized her mindset needed to change. Instead of saying, "I was passed over because I'm a woman," she replaced it with, "I need different experiences to advance." She asked Jake about effective client management strategies, spent more time building relationships in other departments, and enrolled in an online leadership development program. Elena had intentionally shifted her mindset from what held her back to what would move her forward. Eighteen months later, when another management role became available, she landed the position.

Your mind will continue to generate thoughts—helpful, unhelpful, and everything in between. That won't change. But now, you have tools to work with them rather than being overwhelmed by them. (And you also know you don't have to believe every thought you have.) When you pause to get curious, question assumptions, and consider what else might be true (or possible), you're taking back control. You're deciding what deserves your energy, your emotions, and your next move.

Think about it

Recall a recent situation where you felt angry, disappointed, or frustrated. What happened? What self-talk did you notice?

Make a move

Explore other possibilities about "what happened" and choose a new mindset that helps and supports you. Take one action based on your new mindset.

11

Know what you need

Listen to your whole self.

What do you need?

This simple question stumps most women. When asked, they usually struggle to find an answer. It's often because they've never once asked themselves that question. It's also because women are wired—and society expects them—to care for others more than themselves. One unfortunate consequence of this trait is that their own needs tend to get lost in the shuffle, and they seldom learn how to recognize or meet their own needs.

When you're unaware of your needs, you can't express them. When you're unable to express your needs, you can be almost certain they won't be met by you or anyone else. So how do you figure out what you need?

Start by tuning in to the three centers of intelligence we all possess—your head (thoughts), your heart (emotions), and your body (intuition). When you become more aware of what's happening with these centers, you'll become more aware of your needs, which instantly increases the chances they'll be met.

Here's a quick exercise to help you connect with your three centers of intelligence:

Sit quietly in a comfortable spot. Close your eyes, take a few deep breaths to settle in, and then begin quietly reflecting.

> **Head:** What are your thoughts?
>
> Maybe your thoughts are rehashing a difficult conversation from yesterday. Perhaps they're racing ahead to your next meeting. Or your mind is quiet right now. Whatever is happening, just notice.

After about a minute, move your attention to your heart.

> **Heart:** What emotions are you experiencing?
>
> A good starting point is the basic emotions: Are you happy, sad, angry, afraid, surprised, or disappointed? Are you feeling more than one emotion? Notice that.

After a minute or so, shift your attention to your body.

> **Body:** What's happening in your body?
>
> Notice any sensations you're feeling, such as a rapid heartbeat, tension in your temples, or butterflies in your stomach. Or maybe an overall feeling of lightness. Or maybe you can't sense your body right now. (Yes, it happens.) If so, notice that.

After a minute or so, pause. Take a deep breath. Pause.

Now, shift from observing your head, heart, and body to using them as a guide for your needs. Silently ask yourself a question and pay attention to the responses from each center:

> *What do I need?*
>
> Don't rush or force an answer. Allow your awareness to emerge naturally. For example:
>
> Your head might say things like, *I need help. I need more time and money. I need information.*
>
> Your heart might say, *I need companionship. I need to have more fun. I need someone to listen. I need more meaning in my life.*
>
> Your body might say, *I need to eat. I need sleep. I need exercise.*

If this exercise makes you feel awkward or uncomfortable, that's okay. Don't let discomfort discourage you. Do it again tomorrow and then the next day. Each time you do it, it will become easier and more natural. Also, remember that there are no right answers, so avoid trying to change your thoughts, feelings, or sensations during this exercise. Observe them as they are without judgment. Over time, this simple exercise will profoundly enhance your self-awareness and your understanding of your needs.

Once you're clearer on your needs, take action to meet one of them. For example, if you realized through the head/heart/body exercise that your body is tired and you need more sleep, you might decide to go to bed an hour earlier this week. Or maybe one of your needs is to feel more excited about your job; a challenging new assignment would be interesting and motivating. Remember, people can't read your mind. Sometimes you have to ask for what you need. You could say something like this to your manager:

"I've been thinking about what would make me feel excited and fulfilled at work. I realized I need more challenging work. Can you help me get assigned to a high-profile project so I can stretch my skills and work with experts from other departments?"

IRL

Anya was approaching a milestone birthday and expected to feel happy with her husband, nice apartment, and healthy baby. But she felt empty instead. When she agreed to move across the country to support her mate, who was earning more money, she left everything behind, including a job she loved, inspiring coworkers, college friends, and supportive neighbors. Now she was struggling to land a job in a new market with fewer job prospects and no connections, and she was riddled with anxiety and resentment.

After a breakthrough coaching call, Anya realized she had prioritized her family's needs and hadn't articulated her own needs, so they were never considered as part of the overall family plan. When she scanned her needs, she began to understand the source of her unhappiness. Her head was telling her to be grateful for what she had, but her heart showed her how she was losing herself as a result of her family's move. Her body reminded her what it felt like to be energized and excited about her work.

Anya had a candid conversation with her spouse about her need for professional fulfillment and her feelings about sacrificing her interests to support his. The honest exchange made them both more aware and mutually supportive of each other's goals. Now very clear about her objectives, she began networking with confidence to find the full-time role she was looking for.

You are responsible for getting your needs met. Knowing what you need greatly increases the chances that will happen. The hard part is learning how to listen to your whole self—head, heart, and body—but when you do, the reward is worth the effort. Becoming dialed in to these three centers will bring deeper, more immediate self-awareness and, in turn, clarity about your needs. This clarity will allow you to make confident life choices that are your choices. Intentional, not random.

Think about it 

What is one need you have that isn't being met? What is preventing you from meeting this need?

Make a move 

Do one thing today to start meeting that need.

12

Draw lines

When balance is your goal, boundaries are the tool.

When boomers were building their careers 40 years ago, there was zero concept of work-life balance. It was expected that your work was your primary responsibility and your personal life was for you to figure out. Today, employers (mostly) understand that this balance is a critical component of employee retention (which is good for them) and job satisfaction (which is good for you).

But what exactly does it mean? Depending on who you ask, work-life balance could be:

- Equal time spent at work and outside of work
- The ability to tend to personal things during the workday without permission
- Working when it's convenient based on lifestyle needs
- Working the minimum hours required for a fulfilling personal life
- Working for an organization that supports well-being

- Integrating work and life in a way that feels cohesive and flexible

Most people just want to avoid working too much and enjoy a personal life.

But thanks to digital technology, there's now an expectation that you're "always on." Or at least there's an expectation that you can be "on" at any time, whether it's after hours, during the weekend, or when you're on vacation. Where do you find work-life balance when your cell phone and email (and maybe your overbearing manager or needy friend) can find you at any time of the day or night?

This is where boundaries come in.

Think of boundaries as a way to define and communicate what is acceptable and reasonable to you. They help you stay focused on your priorities, manage your time, maintain healthy relationships, and avoid burnout. You could say that boundaries are an often-overlooked form of self-care and a vital tool for creating a work-life balance that works for you. To some degree, boundaries make sustainable success possible.

So how can you draw your lines and effectively communicate them to others?

Assess your situation. This is when knowing what you need gets real. Think about your experience at work and home. What makes you feel good, inside and out? Notice the people or situations that energize or drain you or what causes you to feel resentful or overwhelmed. Those reactions are often signals that your values are being violated and you need to set a boundary. Distinguish between something that happens occasionally (everyone has to work late from time to time) versus a consistent pattern (working late every night for weeks or months).

Boundary needs vary from person to person, but here are some of the most common work-based scenarios that invite boundary setting:

- Late hours at the office

- Working all day without a break
- Lack of flexibility for personal appointments
- Last-minute urgent and nonurgent requests
- Office gossip

Set a boundary. When you're not in charge, it may feel challenging to create and enforce boundaries, but it's possible (and doable!). Here's how:

- Start small with something low risk but meaningful: *"I need to take a lunch break every day."*
- Use "I" statements to underscore your need: *"I need to focus on X right now."*
- Be direct and professional: *"I am uncomfortable discussing my personal life."*
- Avoid sharing unnecessary personal details or apologizing: *"Thank you for understanding."*

As a general rule, boundaries are firm, clear, reasonable, and consistent. And by the way, avoid using the word "boundary" when communicating about one, as it could be perceived as demanding or contentious. A boundary is a good thing, so use positive words to talk about it, such as *"I work best when . . . "* or *"What helps me succeed is . . . "*

Name your nonnegotiables. Everyone's nonnegotiables are different, but here are a few scenarios where holding the line makes sense:

- Someone's request is immoral, unethical, illegal, or harmful to someone else (or you).
- You have a prior commitment that can't be rescheduled.
- You don't have the capacity, or it's not aligned with your responsibilities and priorities.
- Someone's request is unnecessary and can be solved in other ways.
- You are exhausted and need to protect your health and energy.

The hard part of upholding boundaries is getting comfortable saying no. Saying no requires tact, a brief rationale, and a potential alternative solution. If, for example, a colleague from another department is asking you to stay late, you might say something like this:

> *"Thank you for thinking of me. Unfortunately, I'm focused on a number of priorities set by my manager that have demanding deadlines right now. I recommend you check with [person capable of doing the job], who has the skills and might have the capacity."*

Know when to bend. While boundaries are firm, don't be an unscalable wall. Occasionally, you will find it beneficial to be flexible and say yes to a request when it benefits you or a relationship you value.

Yes might be the answer at work when:

- Someone is in a pinch, and only you can help.
- You want to be a team player and earn a return favor.
- It's an opportunity to stretch or learn something new.
- It's an opportunity to work on a high-profile project.
- It's an opportunity to work with a top leader.
- You want to do more to earn more sooner.

Think it over. Don't feel rushed into a decision. If you're not sure if no or yes is the right decision for you, give yourself 24 hours to think about it. And if a full day isn't possible, you might say, "*I am unable to give this my full attention right now. Let me get back to you in an hour.*" This gives you a little time to assess your priorities and respond thoughtfully and unemotionally.

At the end of the day, healthy boundaries are like a good fence—they keep the right things in and the wrong things out, but they still serve as a gate. Don't be afraid to open that gate when something worthwhile comes along, whether it's a stretch assignment, a networking opportunity, or a chance to mentor someone you care about. Boundaries that are too rigid can box you in and limit your opportunities. The objective is to protect your well-being while staying open to the possibilities that help you grow.

IRL

Christie was a high performer at a major omnichannel retailer. In addition to her duties in digital marketing, she was responsible for photo shoots, video production, PR events, and more. After she took on the work of two colleagues who were let go, she found herself working 12-hour days for over a year and multiple hours nearly every weekend. She liked the company, but she was exhausted and couldn't see a way to make the job work much longer.

Christie kept up this insane pace for such a long time that she lost touch with her values. She needed to declare her boundaries to her manager to protect her mental and physical health. Here's what she said:

"I love working for this company. I know I have consistently exceeded expectations and delivered projects on time and under budget. While I'm proud of the impact of my work, I am burning out fast. We need to arrive at a sustainable solution that works for me and the company.

I have three requests: (1) I need to limit my workweek to no more than 45 hours, (2) I can no longer work weekends unless it's an emergency and no other solution is available, and (3) I need someone else to assume responsibility for the administrative tasks that take time away from my core areas of responsibility."

This conversation gave Christie the chance to hit reset with her manager with new boundaries, additional support, and a renewed sense of enthusiasm for her job.

Setting boundaries isn't a onetime decision or conversation. It's an ongoing process. As your career evolves and your personal priorities shift, so, too, will your boundaries. Just remember that you have the power to choose what work-life balance looks like for you. When you draw clear lines that honor both your professional commitments and personal well-being, you won't have to sacrifice one for the other. You can live a whole and satisfying life.

Think about it

What is something important to you at work or at home that requires setting a new boundary? Which boundary do you want to test?

Make a move

Set a boundary for yourself and discuss it with someone it may affect. For example, you might try one of these approaches with your manager:

> *"I'm prioritizing my health by committing to exercising before work. I will be at the office by 9:00 a.m. every morning. When I'm required to be at the office earlier than 9:00 a.m., I will exercise during my lunch hour."*

> *"I share responsibility for caring for my mother in the evenings, so I have to leave the office by 5:00 p.m. each day. If I'm needed after hours, will you let me know in advance so that I can make arrangements for my mother's care?"*

13

Get good with money

Become savvy, not sorry.

Nobody told you that making good money and being good with money are two very different skills.

Managing credit card debt. Getting the right insurance. Tackling your taxes. Signing the lease for a car or apartment. Securing a loan. Building an emergency fund. Making investments.

Do you feel equipped to do all of these things? If not, you're not alone.

For generations, women were denied the ability to control their own finances by a legal system that limited their property rights. And banks wouldn't let women open accounts or get credit cards without their husbands' approval (until the 1970s in the US)—maddening but true! The expectation that men would handle investments, retirement planning, and major financial decisions was deeply ingrained in cultural norms.

This left a financial literacy gap that persists to this day. According to 2023 research conducted by Wells Fargo and The Female Quotient, only 52 percent of women feel comfortable talking about their financial health compared to 62 percent of men. And just 51 percent of women are confident in financial management, compared to 65 percent of men.

In your own life, maybe your parents handled money matters, so you were sheltered from learning the basics. Or you were raised in a culture where discussing money was considered rude or tacky. Or your family got by on very little, so the topic of money was too stress-inducing for your parents and was never discussed with you. Or maybe you had great role models and have developed good money skills (kudos to you!).

No matter your history with money, being money savvy is a choice. It's also one of the most important competencies to have to build the life you want. It's never too late to get good with money. Here's how:

Understand your attitude toward money. Your perspective on money is shaped by your upbringing, cultural influences, personal experiences, and education. All of these can significantly impact the decisions you make and the relationships you form throughout your life. To begin to understand how you think about money, reflect on these five prompts:

- What is the first word that comes to mind when you think about money?
- How would you characterize your attitude about money?
- How comfortable are you talking about money?
- When you were growing up, how was money handled in your family?
- Do you typically have more money than you need, just enough, or not enough?

This thoughtful examination will help you become more attuned to your perspective about money. Identify the things that may be holding you back or that you'd like to change. Maybe you want to think of money as less scary or less scarce. Awareness is the first step toward developing a healthy attitude toward money, one that you can intentionally cultivate.

See money as a tool. Money is often the reward for your hard work. It's also a handy tool—like a Swiss Army knife—that can be used in many ways to positively influence your life and others'. Money can give you peace of mind, alleviate stress, help you take care of your family, and allow you to be generous with others. Money can give you access to resources that make your life easier, more convenient, or more fun.

Respect money. Recognizing that the value of money goes hand in hand with using it responsibly is a key step. For decades, money guru Suze Orman has told people to organize the bills in their wallets and not to toss loose change in their bags. Physically taking care of your money makes you much more conscious of what you have (or don't have). In an increasingly cashless society, it may be hard to feel that tangible connection to your money, but it's still essential. Do you know your cash balance on any given day? Do you know what is owed on your credit card(s)? Do you know your credit score? By being aware of where you stand, you honor the value of every hard-earned dollar.

One more important way to respect money is to stay close to it. Never relinquish control to someone else, whether it's a spouse, partner, or financial advisor. This will ensure you remain in control of your money and long-term financial stability.

Spend with intention. Do you know how much you spend each month? Are you living within your means, or do your bills stress you out? When you align your spending with your values and long-term goals, you spend with intention. An intentional approach reduces consumption anxiety, prevents irrational splurges, and keeps debt manageable.

One way to become more intentional is to establish a personal budget that allows you to live within (or below) your means. Use a budget tracker to manage your spending, prioritize paying off debt, save for emergencies, and invest in your future. Curb your spending impulses with a 24-hour "contemplation period." By waiting one day, you'll buy less stuff you don't need (and we all need less stuff).

Limit lifestyle creep. As you earn more, you'll be inclined to spend more, too. A raise, a bonus, a new job, or debt relief results in more available cash. For most people, that leads to a lifestyle upgrade. Treat yourself; however, be conscious of too much lifestyle creep. Instead, aim to *invest* more rather than spend more when you have extra money. (Your future self will thank you.) Also, periodically review how much you're *actually* spending every month to ensure you remain mindful and within your budget.

Become literate. Money-related topics, such as compensation, insurance, and investments, may be overwhelming. Learn the foundational vocabulary by tapping into educational resources such as financial newsletters, banks, online discussion forums, webinars, podcasts, and an array of personal finance books. Explore the free tools and access to experts at SavvyLadies.org or the Financial Planning Association. Start with personal finance basics to learn how to manage your income and expenses effectively. Consider working with a personal financial advisor to help you understand and achieve your goals. Becoming money literate is a lifelong pursuit, so don't worry about what you don't know yet. Just keep asking questions.

Talk about it. Find your own comfort level discussing money with people close to you or those in a similar life stage. Recognize that their comfort level or financial literacy may differ from yours, so start with simple conversations, like discussing credit scores, contributing to your organization's 401(k), opening a Roth IRA, or setting an emergency savings target. Explore safe, open-ended questions such as, *"When is a splurge worth it?"* or *"What's your top money priority right now?"* Over time, you'll get more comfortable talking about money-related topics, reduce your money-related anxiety, and make better financial decisions.

Protect your earning power. Money may come in at different rates throughout your life. If you decide to leave the full-time workforce, maintain your earning capacity through flexible hours or part-time work. This will help preserve your options down the road. Many people who leave the workforce to raise kids for an extended period are often dismayed by their reduced earning potential when they reenter the workforce. You're not trying to prevent breaks in a career—you're trying to prevent those breaks from unnecessarily limiting your future choices.

IRL

Leslie thought of herself as someone who was "good with money." She had a 401(k), paid her bills on time, and never carried a credit card balance. But somewhere along the way, she let her partner take the lead on most of their financial activities, including managing investments, paying taxes, and budgeting for their future. She told herself it wasn't a big deal and that they were a team. Besides, he liked that stuff more, and she was busy enough with everything else.

One day, late payment notices from the IRS started showing up in their mailbox. At around the same time, her husband lost his job. Suddenly feeling a heap of stress about money, she realized she didn't actually know what their financial situation was. And worse, she didn't know where to start.

Leslie reached out to a friend who was a financial planner and asked for guidance, starting with the basics. The friend enrolled Leslie and her husband into a personal finance course to help them understand their situation and get on a path to stability, transparency, and shared responsibility.

This was a game changer for Leslie. She realized how much she'd been keeping herself at arm's length from important decisions that directly affected her life. And once she got involved, she didn't stop there. She set up regular money check-ins with her husband, tracked their spending, and took an active role in their investments, building security and confidence with each step.

It took some major adjustments in her marriage, but for the first time in a long time, Leslie felt like she was making important choices that would protect her family's future.

Getting good with money is one of the most consequential choices you can make. It puts you in the position to build financial security, weather life's unpredictability, and achieve your long-term aspirations. Most importantly, it lets you live a life where you call the shots.

Think about it 

On a scale of 1 to 10, how would you rate your attitude toward money (1 = unhealthy, 10 = healthy)? On a scale of 1 to 10, how would you rate your spending (1 = unintentional, 10 = intentional)? What do you need to do to move closer to a 10 for each of the questions?

Make a move 

Take one step each week to take control of your personal finances. Continue taking one new step each week to build your competence and confidence with money.

14

Make your trade-offs

There are no perfect choices, only better-informed ones.

There's a reason they say you can't have it all. It's because to have the career and life you want, you have to make trade-offs. For everything you choose to do more of, you have to choose to do less of something else. For everything you want to gain, you sacrifice something else.

Owning your choices requires you to become good at identifying, evaluating, and making your trade-offs. It's especially important because trade-offs impact your time, energy, health, money, and opportunity. Otherwise, you risk being over-scheduled, overwhelmed, fatigued, in debt, or navigating unwelcome adversity (and that stinks).

Trade-offs happen all day, every day. They occur with minor decisions that you may not give a lot of thought to: Will you forgo social media time to expand your IRL social circle by joining a book club? Will you rideshare to work or walk ten blocks to stay within your monthly budget? Will you join your colleagues for drinks or go home early to get extra sleep?

It's tempting to resort to the easiest or most satisfying option in the moment; however, settling for a short-term benefit may impact your longer-term goals. That's not to say you can't enjoy spontaneous moments of delight. Instead, to own your choices, become aware of the consequences of your choices and make your trade-offs with intention.

When the consequences of your choices are minor, the trade-offs are usually less substantial and easier to weigh. When the consequences involve significant time, money, or effort, the trade-offs require more thorough consideration. These choices and trade-offs may feel daunting, especially when they impact big life stuff, such as where you live, an important relationship, or which job you take.

For example, investment banking is known for long hours, weekends, and grueling deadlines. So what's the attraction? The sector typically pays extremely well, is perceived as stable, and has cachet. Working in this industry is a choice that comes with trade-offs, notably little time for a personal life.

In contrast, choosing to work for a start-up may be a great experience working directly with founders, having lots of responsibility, and receiving stock options that could be life changing. The trade-off is that most start-ups have little structure, few established processes, and a below-market salary that may not pay off if the company doesn't go public, get sold, or experience big growth.

If you choose to go back to school full time to earn an advanced degree, you forgo earning a salary during that period. If you choose to go to school while working full time, you will experience long hours with little time for friends, but you'll end up with an advanced degree that might catapult your career.

When contemplating the trade-offs of a decision, look at these key considerations:

Short term: Does the trade-off satisfy a crucial short-term need? If so, it might be easy to make the trade-off because you're getting something important that you need now.

Long term: Does the trade-off move you closer to your long-term goal? These are the hardest trade-offs to make because your goal is in the distant future and the payoff isn't immediate. However, they may also be the trade-offs that benefit you the most over time.

Change: Is the trade-off permanent, or can it be reversed? If the trade-off can be modified when your circumstances change, it's a simpler trade-off to make.

Risk tolerance: How much can you afford to lose without it affecting your daily life? The more people are depending on you financially (e.g., kids or other family members), the less risk you can comfortably take. The fewer immediate financial obligations you have, the more you can afford to invest in higher-risk, higher-reward options. Your tolerance for risk may change as you move through different stages of your life.

Opportunity cost: What are you giving up by making this trade-off? Is the upside of the gain more valuable to you than the downside of the loss or sacrifice? (This is not always easy to answer, so really think about this.) Sometimes you're choosing between good and better options, sometimes between good and necessary, and sometimes between bad and worse. The discomfort often comes from wanting to avoid the trade-off entirely, but that's not realistic.

Most trade-off decisions don't improve with endless deliberation. Give yourself a reasonable time frame to gather information and weigh options, then commit to choosing. Perfect information rarely exists, and waiting for it often becomes its own costly trade-off.

IRL

Samantha had numerous offers after graduating at the top of her class in business school. She could be a sales rep for a top pharmaceutical company that was offering a strong compensation package with little risk. She could join classmates as a cofounder of a tech-based start-up that provides emergency evacuation solutions. Or she could be the co-owner of a bowling alley funded by a local multimillionaire who was looking for an entrepreneurial young partner to help them transform a dated business into a happening entertainment venue that could be sold relatively quickly.

So many choices! All had promising upsides, yet all had downsides, too. The pharmaceutical company had a good salary and flexible hours, but it was a values clash. The start-up could be fun and exciting to do with friends, but it would require asking family for funding and living at home. Samantha wasn't a bowler, so the bowling alley option was not initially interesting to her. But the owner offered a compelling opportunity to learn about operations, grow a business, earn a good salary, and be an owner with a share of the profits, without investing any of her own money. This option had very little risk. It was a highly motivating proposition with a trade-off of long hours for two years.

Samantha went with the bowling alley. She turned it into a vibrant gathering spot and doubled its profits. After the business was sold, Samantha earned a hefty sum that gave her the freedom to travel before exploring her next opportunity.

Most choices come with trade-offs that either move you toward or away from your goals. And the ones you're willing to make will depend on your life stage, responsibilities, and priorities. The discomfort of weighing these decisions never entirely disappears, but your confidence will grow with practice. Ten years from now, you won't remember most of the small trade-offs you agonized over, but you will remember the big ones you made with intention and courage. Those are the decisions that create the life you want to live.

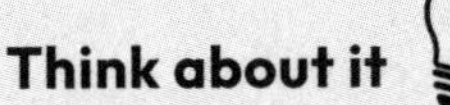

Think about it

What choice are you currently facing that relates to an important goal in your life? What are the trade-offs?

Make a move

After evaluating the trade-offs, make a decision.

PART 2
WRAP UP

The journey to owning your choices starts with a single decision—the decision to stop waiting for permission, perfect timing, or someone else to make things happen for you. When you own your choices, you take full responsibility for your career and your life. You are in charge of your destiny. You'll exercise your own agency. The people in your life will respect your self-assuredness and determination. And you'll be in the driver's seat of the fulfilling life you have chosen.

- **Control what you can control** and focus your energy on what you can change or influence.
- **Manage your mindset** to create supportive mental frameworks that help you.
- **Know what you need** to increase the chances of your needs being met.
- **Draw lines** to establish boundaries that create your work-life balance.
- **Get good with money** to build financial security and the life you want.
- **Make your trade-offs** in an informed and deliberate way to support your goals.

Choose your crew

Who's your crew? Maybe they're your childhood besties or friends you made during college or while at various jobs. Maybe there's a neighbor, sibling, or another relative in the mix. Or someone you know from the dog park or your kid's after-school program. Now that you're picturing your people, ask yourself this: How do they add value to your life?

Your crew is vital to your overall well-being. That's why you need a crew who lifts you up, who's there for you on good and bad days, and serves as your most trusted support system. The people in your inner circle can have a huge influence on the quality of your life. They *get* you.

So be choosy about who's in your crew.

Have a small but mighty circle. A few deep friendships will have a greater impact on you than a large group of acquaintances. Whether it's someone you interact with every day or only talk to occasionally, you just know they're one of your people because when you're together, you feel connected, appreciated, and understood. The members of your little crew are the people you count on most. They are also good listeners, support you through difficult times, and celebrate your wins. And you do the same for them. But no one keeps score.

Let them ebb and flow. Some close friendships develop during important life stages and stay strong across time and distance. You'll notice that these important relationships go through phases as your life changes. New cities. New jobs. New partners or kids. All of these life moves create space in relationships. Allow those relationships to breathe without letting them wither. With occasional efforts to stay in touch, you'll discover that the close bonds may be quickly reignited, so your connection is never lost, just loosened.

Break up, too. You may find you no longer share common interests with some longtime friends. Or you may discover that one or both of you have changed, and you have grown apart. If your relationship is not benefiting both of you, let it fall away. No need for a dramatic ending. Just appreciate it for what it was and move on. Not every friendship lasts a lifetime. Let your crew evolve as you evolve.

The people closest to you help shape who you become and how you experience life's journey. So choose an awesome crew!

Choose love, too

The secret to everything you want in life isn't found on your résumé or in your bank account. It's learning to give and receive love—and knowing that you deserve both.

So how can you dial into the love you deserve and have to offer?

Love yourself. Start with the relationship you'll have the longest: the one you have with yourself. When you truly love yourself, everything changes. You treat yourself like someone worth caring for, and you take care of yourself. Your whole self. You practice self-compassion—the gentle acknowledgment that you're human, imperfect, and deserving of kindness, especially from yourself. You stop shrinking to fit into spaces too small for you. You worry less about what others think and focus more on what you think. You have more love to give because you feel freer to give it. Your tank is full instead of running on empty.

Love well. When you love yourself, you naturally draw in people who genuinely want to be with you. As you develop romantic relationships—whether you date, partner, or marry—be mindful of how you show up and influence the dynamic. Be a person who demonstrates vulnerability, openness, patience, and healthy boundaries. Choose to see people fully without trying to fix or change them. Make room for your differences. But remember that loving well isn't loving without limits; it's loving with wisdom.

Create space for others to be human while protecting what's sacred in yourself. Be generous but not reckless, loyal but not blind. You can love someone deeply while refusing to accept behavior that harms you or them.

Loving well lays the foundation for healthy, equitable, and lasting relationships. This strong foundation helps you to communicate effectively, manage conflict, share responsibilities, and pursue your dreams—both individually and collectively.

Look for important love clues. You're more likely to find love if you know what to look for. Love clues are a lot of little things that add up to big things, such as eye contact that makes you feel truly seen, as if you're the most important person in that moment. Overlapping values that provide common ground to build from. Respect they show you and others—in the beginning and over time. Genuine excitement when you share your desires and ambitions. Thoughtful gestures that demonstrate a warm heart and kindness. When you choose them as much as they choose you. This is when love flourishes.

With love, your life gets bigger, better, and richer. Go get some.

Part 3

FIND YOUR FIT

'FESS UP REST UP

UP SKILL UP POWER

POWER UP STAND

UP RAMP UP GEAR

PUMP UP 'FESS UP

UP OPEN UP RISE

STEP UP LIFT UP

MOVE UP FIRE UP

SHOW UP LEVEL UP

SPEAK UP MOVE

'FESS UP REST UP

UP SKILL UP POWER

POWER UP STAND

When you discover a cool pair of shoes on sale from a brand you love, it's hard to pass them up, even if they're a half size too small. But the first time you wear them, you realize they're giving you blisters and pinching your toes. Even if you really love these shoes, eventually you'll push them to the back of your closet and reach for the ones that feel good. When it comes to shoes, fit matters.

Fit matters at work, too. For an employer, fit means you jibe with the organizational culture, you perform well, and you get along with your colleagues. If you're a good fit, they think they've made a great hire, and they want to keep you. Fit is so important to employers that they systematically assess candidates and employees for fit. For example, they evaluate whether the employee's skills, experience, attitude, and compensation requirements align with the position. In this transactional relationship between employee and employer, the employer is usually actively assessing for fit.

But what about you? Who's thinking about whether a job or an organization is a good fit for you? Here's the thing—that's your responsibility. Yet as important as fit is to an employee's job satisfaction, it's surprising how many people don't give much thought to it. Why is this? One reason is that a good fit might seem like a luxury. Sometimes when you have bills to pay, a job might be all about the paycheck—hey, we've all been there. Another reason is that while you may think about fit occasionally, you're unsure how to evaluate it beyond how you feel on a given day. It's not discussed or written about from an employee's perspective, so there are few, if any, reference points. Let's change that.

What does fit mean to you?

For you, fit means that the culture aligns with your values, you're supported to succeed and grow in your role, you're fairly compensated, and you enjoy what you do and the people you work with. If it's a good fit for you, the role and the organization suit you, and you want to stay.

What does a good fit feel like at work?

When your job is a good fit, going to work is something you look forward to. You believe that what you're doing is meaningful. You feel a sense of belonging and connection with your organization without changing yourself to fit in. The job is challenging, you have opportunities to grow, and the work environment is conducive to how you work best. You have crap days like anyone else, but it's easy enough to turn the page tomorrow.

A good fit doesn't mean a perfect fit. Even in a job you love, some aspects of fit will be good while others aren't as good. Or the job or the organization may evolve, and aspects of fit that used to be good may not feel so good anymore. Or you may evolve, and what worked well for you in the past is no longer right. Fit can change and perfect isn't the objective. Knowing what fits you is what you're looking for.

If you're in a job that's a bad fit, you know it. Maybe you're out of sync with your manager. Or you're uncomfortable with the way your organization does business. Or you're spending most of your time on work you weren't hired to do. Or all of the above. Just like when you're wearing those pinchy shoes, all you can think about is making the bad feelings go away. This is when people often start looking for another job or dial back their effort and "quiet quit."

When struggling at work, most people ask themselves the wrong question: "Should I stay or should I go?" But this question limits your possibilities to a mere two options. A better, more powerful question to ask yourself is this: "Why am I here, and how can I grow?" Answering *that* question may lead you to countless options and empower you to take responsibility for what you need and want. And knowing what fits you will positively impact your career—in the short and long term. For example, your most valuable professional relationships and job opportunities will likely flow from your best professional experiences. So working on fit is well worth your effort.

Fit wasn't something I thought much about early in my career. I showed up, worked hard, and hoped it would all work out.

At age 31, I joined a small technology communications company. I eagerly said yes to the opportunity because I'd be working directly with the CEO to develop my new role as a strategist. My enthusiasm for the new job quickly hit a wall, however, when my colleagues made it clear I wasn't welcome. They seemed put off by my lack of a published job description and the fact that my position was never posted for other people to consider.

I hadn't met any of my colleagues during the interview process, so they knew nothing about me. Further, I wasn't formally or informally onboarded to the company, so I didn't know who did what or how the company operated. As a result, nobody knew my role or capabilities. This meant I wasn't assigned to client projects. I felt frustrated and bored.

For the first year, I was isolated and miserable. My colleagues went to lunch each day without inviting me to join, and they excluded me from their team holiday gift exchange. While I had the trust and support of the CEO, I just couldn't get any traction with my peers.

It was a great company, but something felt off. I was tempted to bail. Leaving would have been the easiest choice, but I didn't have a résumé prepared or another job lined up, so I decided to dig in and stay put.

First, I reminded myself that I had taken the job because it offered me the chance to be a pioneer in an emerging field. I also realized my boss hadn't set me up for success with my coworkers, so I would have to approach them differently. To change their perception of me, I needed to show up differently. Instead of angst, frustration, and impatience, I would demonstrate determination, helpfulness, and initiative. And respect. I would earn their respect over time by giving them my respect now.

Given my planning and design background with leading retail brands, I set my sights on winning a big retail client, which would be a departure from the company's technology-oriented client roster. It was an audacious goal, yet I felt emboldened by the possibility and the challenge. I got the CEO's green light to lead a significant research initiative that helped us get smarter about digital retail trends, form insightful strategies, and develop creative concepts to propose to prospective clients. The process required working with many of my colleagues across the organization. After over a year of ideating, pitching, and competing, we landed a big-name client. Along the way, I was able to showcase my strengths, bring positive energy, and build trust and respect with my colleagues.

After months of intentional effort, I finally found my fit and built a career with this company for many years.

Ultimately, only you can determine what a good fit feels like for you. Only you can evaluate fit based on what's important to you. And only you can advocate for fit in your current or future jobs. When you have a clear understanding of what a good fit is for you, you can spot what you're looking for, what's lacking in your job, or what you want in your next one. You can also make smart moves to improve your fit. If it works, you've improved your work experience. And if it doesn't, you'll know you've done everything possible to fix your fit before jumping ship.

Find your fit. You deserve one that lifts you *up*!

15

Size things up

Assess all the dimensions of fit.

When things feel off kilter at work, why is it so hard to put your finger on the reason?

While employers use algorithms and fancy frameworks to determine whether you're a fit for them, it's unlikely that you're methodically thinking about fit yourself. That's because it's a squishy topic, and there hasn't been an easy way to do so—until now. Equipt Women collaborated with experts in talent and workplace culture to create a simple Work Fit Framework to assess fit from your perspective, not the organization's. Workplace fit occurs along these four key dimensions:

- **You:** How you perform
- **Your role:** The current and future scope of the job
- **The environment:** Other factors that impact you
- **The organization:** Values, culture, and stability

Before diving into the details of each dimension, there are a few guiding principles to help you know how and when to use this Work Fit Framework. First, know that not all dimensions of fit are necessarily of equal importance. Depending on your career stage and life circumstances, each dimension may have varying significance to you at any given time.

Also, there's no one time to use this framework. You can use it at any point in your career. However, a fit assessment is particularly useful when you feel stuck or when things aren't going well. It can also serve as a periodic wellness check to help you distinguish between an occasional bad day and a series of recurring ones. For example, a one-off project requiring long hours for a few days differs from projects that are routinely underresourced and lead to burnout.

Finally, don't overanalyze the first few months in a new role or with a new organization, as there's always an adjustment period. And don't blame yourself if you've landed in a bad situation. It's simply something to improve or resolve.

With those guiding principles in mind, consider the four dimensions of fit in more detail.

You: How you perform

It starts with you. The first dimension of fit is your performance, which is mostly within your control. It's about taking responsibility to bring your best, connecting with other people, and tapping into the available resources designed to support you. This dimension is humming when you can:

- Bring a positive attitude and a willingness to learn
- Be your authentic self
- Employ the skills required in the role
- Meet deadlines and expectations
- Show initiative

- Build relationships
- Seek feedback and support
- Communicate effectively with your manager
- Utilize the organization's tools and support systems
- Make your work matter

When you perform well, you improve yourself, others, and the work. This builds your reputation as respected, dependable, and sought after (which feels great). Over time, it leads to better assignments, more visibility with leadership, and recognition. (This feels even greater.) Most importantly, being a high performer gives you leverage, which is beneficial during annual reviews, promotion cycles, project staffing, or organizational restructuring.

If you're not performing well, why is that? Be honest with yourself. It's the only way this framework will be helpful. If you're struggling with some aspects of the "you" dimension, consider asking your manager for support. If that's a dead end, perhaps the *role* is not a fit for you.

Your role: The current and future scope of the job

The second dimension of fit is your role. Assess whether the role aligns with your values, makes you feel appreciated, and provides a skills match with growth potential. The role is a good fit when you are:

- Energized, challenged, and look forward to your work
- Doing work that is compatible with your values
- Developing new skills
- Applying your strengths most of the time
- Respected by your teammates
- Fairly compensated
- Clear about a path for upward mobility
- Working for a great boss

When you're in a role that fits, you experience "flow," where time seems to disappear because you're so engaged. The work feels invigorating, and you're eager to continue learning new skills and expanding your knowledge. You're more likely to feel fulfilled by your work and take pride in your professional identity. You become more driven to excel without needing external motivation or pressure.

Conversely, nothing is more frustrating than doing your best to perform, but something is still lacking or problematic with the job. You might be in over your head or simply in a role that isn't well suited for you. There may be a lack of fit with the role if you are:

- Assigned many tasks that distract you from your core responsibilities
- Stretched well beyond your capabilities, causing costly errors
- Experiencing unmanageable stress
- Bored
- Not applying your strengths most of the time
- On an unsupportive team
- Working with an unsupportive or lousy manager
- Underpaid relative to your responsibilities

Finding a role that fits you is essential to your health and happiness. It leads to less burnout, higher job satisfaction, and greater overall life satisfaction.

The environment: Other factors that impact you

Another important dimension of fit is the environment you work in. This encompasses the conditions that impact your overall work experience, including how, when, and where you work. When assessing this dimension of fit, consider whether you feel comfortable—physically, emotionally, and psychologically—to perform at your best. The environment is a good fit when you have:

- A workspace that meets your needs (space, lighting, acoustics)
- An arrangement that works best for you (in-office, remote, hybrid)

- Some autonomy in how you work
- Flexibility with your schedule
- One or more friends as colleagues
- A sense of inclusion and belonging
- The tools and resources to perform your job effectively
- A positive response to or energy from the workplace vibe
- The ability to successfully integrate your work and life

The right environment feels good and creates a virtuous cycle where your well-being enables better performance. This, in turn, leads to more opportunities, more happiness, and more job satisfaction.

The organization: Values, culture, and stability

The final dimension of fit is the organization. You have the least control over this dimension, so making a good choice is crucial. Think about what the organization represents, the culture it cultivates, how it communicates, and how it develops and rewards its employees. The organization is a good fit when:

- Its values are exhibited in employees' day-to-day behavior
- One or more of its core values are compatible with yours
- You receive frequent and open communication
- Its mission is inspiring to you
- You trust the leadership
- It's financially stable
- You're proud to work there
- It has competitive benefits
- It offers professional development
- It provides opportunities for upward mobility
- It has fair and transparent pay policies, and you feel valued

Since this is where you'll spend most of your waking hours, make sure it works for you. The organization reflects on your reputation through association, so be mindful of what they represent. It will also influence your network, earnings, and the trajectory of your career in the years and decades ahead. Make sure you're choosing them as much as they're choosing you.

IRL

Janelle worked at a large, global nonprofit and felt passionate about the organization's mission and its ability to positively impact the lives of children. She loved her role as the operations director, which allowed her to lead big projects and collaborate with teammates around the world. She knew she was considered a high performer by her organization because she received consistently positive feedback and a top rating in her annual reviews.

But despite her strong performance, Janelle felt increasingly frustrated at work. Her new boss, who had joined the company earlier in the year, had a management style that clashed with how she worked best. He was the definition of a micromanager—he reviewed her work line by line, asked for constant updates, and insisted on being looped in on every email.

At first Janelle hoped the intense oversight would ease up after he got used to his job, but six months in, the situation had gotten worse. She was drowning in status updates and producing extensive documentation for making the smallest of decisions. She no longer felt trusted to do her job. To find a workable solution, Janelle suggested more frequent check-ins and daily progress summaries to keep him updated. She even asked her boss directly, "How can we work better together so that you get the information you need and I have the latitude to get things done efficiently?"

He said he preferred to be "in the trenches with the team" and suggested she get used to his style. When he made it clear he was unwilling to make adjustments, she knew their incompatibility problem wasn't going away.

Within a few months, Janelle found an opportunity to transition to a different team in her organization that was led by a senior leader known for giving people autonomy in their roles. This new job was a much better fit to her work style and overall happiness at work.

You now have a framework to systematically and holistically assess your work circumstances. It will help you identify what's working and what's not and begin to explore ways to proactively strengthen your fit. Remember, work fit isn't fixed—it changes as you grow and your circumstances change. The clearer you are about what a good fit means for you, the better decisions you'll make regarding where to dedicate your time and energy. Trust your instincts and remember that you deserve to thrive at work, not just survive it.

Think about it

Reflecting on all the jobs you've had so far—from your first job to your current one—where did you experience the best fit? What made the fit good for you?

Make a move

Evaluate each of the four dimensions of fit at your current organization using a scale of 1 to 5 (1 = weak and 5 = strong). Identify which dimension of fit is the most important to you and which dimension you want to be stronger.

16

Make your work matter

Meaning is the ultimate motivator.

You're likely to spend 90,000 hours of your life working—more than anything else you will do except sleeping. The simple equation of work is this: You give your employer your time, and they give you money.

But there ought to be more to all those hours you clock on the job than just a paycheck. To feel great about your work, it needs to matter to you. It's gotta have meaning.

Meaning occurs when what you're doing feels significant and worthwhile. It connects what you care about, what you do, and the organization you work for. When you find meaning in what you do, your job provides personal as well as professional satisfaction, which is what makes meaning such an important contributor to fit.

According to a 2021 McKinsey report, 70 percent of employees say that when their work feels meaningful, they perform better, are more committed, and are less likely to go looking for a new job. The search for meaning at work is especially important to younger generations. A 2025 Deloitte report found that 44 percent of Gen Zers and 45 percent of millennials have left a role because it lacked purpose, with nearly 9 out of 10 saying that having a sense of purpose at work is "very or somewhat important" to their job satisfaction.

There are a number of factors that may be meaningful to you at work:

The organization. Are you proud to work for your organization? Are you aligned with what your organization stands for, how it conducts business, and how it treats its employees? Are you energized by the strategies it has prioritized?

The impact you have. Think about how your work contributes to something bigger than you. Maybe you are helping solve problems that are important to you. Do you have the opportunity to lead a challenging project or to impact the organization's bottom line? Does your work improve other people's lives or make a difference in your community or elsewhere in the world?

Your relationships. Do you respect and admire the people you work with? Do they share your values and genuinely care about you as a person? Are you learning from a dynamic and inspiring leader? Do you have a good rapport with customers or other outside stakeholders? Strong relationships make work more fulfilling, even when the tasks themselves aren't exciting.

The skills you're building. What professional development programs or stretch assignments do you have access to? Are you able to grow skills that position you for future opportunities?

Your values. Are your values reflected in your daily activities or interactions? Your values help you make decisions, recognize what's missing, and adjust your path. You can use them to connect to an intrinsic motivator. For example, if you value

- **Creativity:** Seek opportunities to innovate, develop new products or services, or solve problems in novel ways.
- **Integrity:** Advocate for ethical decision-making, policymaking, or transparent communication.
- **Growth:** Pursue sales, business development, launching new products, or continuous learning.
- **Community:** Build strong relationships with colleagues and customers, mentor others, or become a team leader.
- **Impact:** Link your daily tasks to broader organizational or societal goals that make other people's lives better.
- **Environmental stewardship:** Look for opportunities to protect ecological systems, preserve biodiversity, or develop regenerative solutions.

You will feel focused and energized when you find meaning in your work. Relish that feeling and stay attuned to it. As time passes and life changes, the source of meaning in your work may change. If meaning is lacking in your current situation, this is a red flag that you may have a fit problem that needs your attention.

IRL

After college, Sarah joined a nonprofit where she led a fellowship program that paired student engineers with people who have disabilities to design real-world tech solutions. While the salary wasn't great, it was enough to support her lifestyle and to (finally) move out of her parents' home. It was her first full-time job, and she had her hands in everything from program management and partnerships to fundraising and social media.

She thoroughly enjoyed the diversity of her tasks, but what made the work meaningful was the impact she was having. Every day, she could see firsthand that the tools these students were building were making people's lives easier and safer. Sarah felt proud knowing her work was helping to make that happen.

Even though she usually worked remotely, Sarah developed strong relationships with her team. She felt respected, trusted, and supported, especially when decisions had to be made quickly. Being valued and having an impact, combined with the mission of the work itself, gave her a powerful sense of purpose and belonging.

Finding meaning at work isn't about waiting for your dream job to land in your lap. It's about actively looking for ways to connect your current role with what matters most to you. Sometimes meaning emerges gradually as your relationships deepen or you take on new challenges. Sometimes it requires making intentional changes to how you approach your work or where you focus your energy. The key is to stay open to discovering meaning in unexpected places. When you find it, you'll know—work stops feeling like something you're required to do and starts feeling like something you can't wait to do. And that changes everything.

Think about it 

Which aspects of your work are meaningful to you? Which aspects of your work would you like to have more meaning?

Make a move 

Try doing something different this week to find more meaning in your work. It could relate to what you're working on, who you're collaborating with, or how you feel about your work.

17

Know your value

Use facts, not feelings.

Even when everything else about your job seems nearly ideal for you, if you suspect your compensation doesn't reflect your value to the organization, that pinchy-shoe, bad-fit feeling will nag at you and distract you.

Receiving fair compensation is a massive contributor to fit, not just because it relates to the money deposited into your account every pay period. It's also because it's a reflection of your organization's respect for you and what you contribute, as well as your respect for yourself. This is why compensation is such an emotional, hot-potato topic when it should just be about basic math.

To evaluate whether your compensation contributes positively or negatively to your job fit, you have to know the fair market value of your work. If you don't know that figure off the top of your head, you're not alone. Most people don't know this information. A 2022 Gartner survey revealed that only 32 percent of workers feel they're paid fairly.

Feel? Fair compensation is not something you feel. It's something you need to know.

Your fair market value is what you should expect to earn in your role relative to your peers across your organization, industry, and location. When it comes to compensation, knowledge is power. Knowing (or not knowing) your value early in your career may have significant long-term effects. For example, being underpaid by $5k beginning in your 20s could amount to $540k in unrealized earnings over 25 years (at 8 percent compounded annually). That's a lot of dough left on the table! And that doesn't even factor in lost earnings from unrealized future raises.

Don't assume or try to guess your value. You can't. *You must do your homework.* When you do, you'll have a solid reference point and leverage for future salary discussions.

Look at comparables. Research compensation for similar roles, responsibilities, industries, organization size, and geography. These are all relevant factors for the most reliable comparisons. Tap free online resources such as Payscale, Indeed, Glassdoor, Fishbowl, Teamblind, LinkedIn, AI platforms, and Salary.com. Seek out insight from recruiters and search for pay studies from professional organizations that publish compensation-related information.

Review the pay band. Ask HR (or your manager) for the pay range for your role (usually referred to as a pay band). Most medium and large organizations make pay band information public or provide it to employees on request. If this information is not provided, ask your manager where you are in the pay band relative to the midpoint. If you are new to the role, you are likely at the lower end of the pay band; if you're experienced in the role and performing well, you may be in the middle; and if you've been exceeding expectations for an extended period, you should be at or near the top of the pay band. If your organization does not use pay bands, your external research will be even more important.

Ask industry peers. If you know people in a similar role with similar responsibilities, industry, organization size, and geography, ask them. If you don't, search for peers on

LinkedIn and send them a message. You could say, *"I am researching compensation for my role, which seems to be similar to yours. I've been in this role for three years, and the pay range for my position is $X to $Y. Can you tell me if this range is consistent with your experience?"* For salaries below $100k, use a 10 percent range below (X) and above (Y) your salary. For example, if your salary is $80k, suggest a range of $72k to $88k. If the salary is above $100k, use a 15 percent range. If you get a response to your request for information, ask for a brief phone call to discuss more details, such as bonuses and other pay-related perks.

Ask your colleagues. Compensation may be an uncomfortable topic to discuss. That's why many people (especially women) choose not to talk about it at all, even with close friends. However, not talking about it may hold you back. If you're in an environment where you trust your coworkers, ask them if they are willing to confidentially share salary data to help each other. Historically, this was uncommon (even prohibited in many organizations), but internal benchmarks are one of the best ways to know if your employer is fairly compensating you. Many employers frown upon employees sharing salary information, but younger generations are increasingly challenging the traditional taboo. It might be tricky to navigate these conversations, however, because they can cause resentment or stir up office conflict. Make it a private, professional conversation focused on understanding the industry standard. Try something like this:

> *"I'm trying to get a better sense of compensation ranges for our type of role. Would you be comfortable sharing a general range of what you're making? I'm happy to share mine too."*
>
> *"I'm preparing for my annual salary review and want to make sure I'm fairly compensated. What insights do you have regarding what people in similar roles earn here?"*
>
> *"I think we could both benefit from understanding the compensation landscape better. Would you be interested in confidentially sharing salary info? It could help us both in future negotiations."*

Compile your research. Combine the information you've gathered to determine your market value. Look for consistent patterns across your research. Recognize that the same title may vary in scope or expectations, so try to be as specific as possible. Also, compensation philosophies may vary across organizations and industries, with some organizations offering benefits packages that increase the value of total compensation. Therefore, making an apples-to-apples comparison might be challenging. Even if you can't compare the exact role across many organizations of a similar size and geography, you'll find a general compensation range that is still useful. The bottom line is that it's rarely a clear-cut situation, but doing your research will help you be better informed so you can be a stronger self-advocate.

All of this homework provides concrete evidence of your market value rather than relying on assumptions or guesswork. You may find you're fairly compensated—if so, great! Now you have confirmation that your employer values your contributions appropriately, which is a positive sign of one dimension of fit. You could also discover you're overpaid, which is valuable information, too. It might indicate that your employer really wants to keep you or your skills are in high demand, or it might explain why your raise was small last year. You may find that you're underpaid. If so, now you have the facts, not just a feeling. This research becomes the foundation for future conversations about compensation and helps you make informed decisions about fit.

IRL

Lauren excelled in her job at a global tech company and was respected by her colleagues. She received annual merit increases and bonuses, which made her feel appreciated until she discovered that men in the company with less experience and in positions two levels below her were earning considerably more than she did.

Outraged by what she felt was unfair, her first instinct was to quit. After taking a few deep breaths, however, she recognized that acting out of emotion was not going to advance her cause. She decided to get more information before doing anything rash. After researching compensation for her role internally and externally, she was shocked and disappointed to learn she was being underpaid by nearly 30 percent.

Calmly and professionally, Lauren presented her research findings to her manager and HR. She also provided a detailed account of her performance over the last three years, including the accolades she had received from colleagues and executive leadership. With a clear understanding of what she ought to be earning in her role, she requested a salary adjustment that reflected her proven value to the company. The company responded by increasing her base salary and bumping up her bonus percentage, which put her on par with her peers.

When you do your homework, you become more informed about the compensation you deserve. Whether that leads to a productive conversation with your manager, a strategic job search, or simply the peace of mind that comes from knowing you're valued appropriately, you'll be operating from a position of strength. When you know you're paid fairly, you feel pretty freakin' good, too!

Think about it 

Do you know the fair market value of your work?

Make a move 

Collect at least five benchmarks to determine if you're being fairly compensated (or not).

18

Land a great boss

Follow a true leader.

Sometimes *what* you do is not as important as *who* you do it with.

A great boss cares about you as an individual, exposes you to bigger and better opportunities, invests in your growth, gives constructive feedback, and advocates for your upward mobility. A great boss is another disproportionate contributor to fit. If you have one, you may (wisely) overlook other aspects of fit that are lacking.

A great boss exposes you to their network, includes you in meetings that you might otherwise not have been invited to, gives you stretch assignments, generously shares their knowledge, and guides your career path. They teach you how the business operates and makes money. They provide glowing endorsements or referrals and bring you along as they move up or move on.

Why would your boss do all of these things? It's good for them, too. They want to lead a strong team they can trust and grow. With a strong team, they can have a greater impact in their own role in the organization. It's also rewarding for a great boss to see their team flourish.

You may have had your share of not-so-great bosses. These people often have had little leadership training, are in a job that's too big for their skill set, or lack time for or interest in team building. They usually don't see their job as helping you to be successful because you work for them. As a result, they won't mentor you, provide useful feedback, or advocate on your behalf. And they are one of the top reasons people leave their jobs. The upside is that they provide an unforgettable portrait of who you don't want to work for or become!

When you accept a new job with a new organization, fate usually determines whether you land a good boss. If your new boss is great, you hit the jackpot. Seriously. But if they're not great, you're going to feel it. And when you do, you will certainly wonder whether this job is a good fit for you. If you discover your new boss is really horrible, you might be tempted to look for another job immediately. But heading for the exit isn't your only option. You may not have a great boss now, but there may be great bosses elsewhere in your organization. You just need to know how to spot a great boss, then find a way to work with them. Here's how:

Observe. Identify the leaders in your organization who:

- Are respected by others, especially their team
- Acknowledge other people's contributions
- Invite diverse perspectives to be heard
- Are dynamic and inspiring
- Navigate conflict well
- Advocate for their team
- Have a life outside of work

Get closer. Get to know one or more of these leaders by:

- Requesting to work on a project with which they're involved
- Attending their presentations, speeches, or office hours
- Responding to their digital posts on LinkedIn or on the organization's intranet
- Asking them to meet for coffee to learn about their career journey and share your interest in working with them

Take action. At the first opportunity, apply for an open role on their team. If you score an interview, be prepared with thoughtful questions to assess if they'd be a great boss for you:

- What value motivates you most each day?
- How do you help your team members grow professionally?
- What's your approach to team conflict?
- How do you handle mistakes on your team?
- What success metrics do you use for your team?
- How do you approach work-life balance?
- How do you give and seek feedback?
- How do you celebrate team wins?

Pay attention. Good questions reveal a lot; however, there is no foolproof way to know if someone will be a great boss until you work together. Notable red flags to watch out for when you're getting to know them or interviewing with them might be if they:

- Speak negatively about current or past employees
- Spend most of the time talking about themselves
- Don't acknowledge the contributions of team members
- Don't seem to enjoy the people part of being a manager
- Seem disinterested in your career aspirations
- Give vague or curt answers

IRL

Melissa was a high performer in a biotech company but didn't enjoy working for her boss, who didn't care to invest in her growth and rarely provided feedback. She saw that other leaders in the company gave public kudos to their teams, advocated for them to get high-profile project assignments, and gave them access to professional development training.

Melissa wanted to work for someone who believed in her and was rooting for her success. But she needed to tread carefully. Her boss might be hurt or angry when Melissa told her she wanted to leave the team. Yet Melissa knew she'd need a reference from her boss to transition to another role in the organization. In her next one-on-one with her manager, Melissa explained that she wanted to learn another part of the business so she could be more valuable to the company over the long term. Her manager agreed to support Melissa and provide a reference as long as she committed to helping find and train her replacement.

From there, Melissa emailed a leader she admired in another department to express her admiration for their leadership style and value to the company, and to ask to be considered for an open role on their team. With her manager's endorsement, she was invited to interview and ultimately landed the job and a great boss.

A great boss will be an asset to you today and shape the trajectory of your career for years to come. Their commitment to your growth will compress years of learning into months for you. They will inspire you to perform at the highest level and advocate for your advancement. Don't leave this to chance. Start observing leaders in your organization today, get to know the ones who impress you, and position yourself to work with people like them. Your career will thank you.

Who do you admire in your current (or another) organization who could be a great boss?

Make a move

Write a compelling email to this potential great boss to introduce yourself and request a brief meeting to get acquainted and share your interest in working with them in the future.

> *Hello [Name],*
>
> *I'm [Your Name] from [Your Department]. I've been following your work on [specific project] and admire how you've [specific leadership quality you've observed].*
>
> *I'm always looking to learn from strong leaders in our organization. Would you have 15 minutes for a quick coffee to discuss your career journey and share insights about [relevant topic]?*
>
> *I'm flexible with timing and happy to meet at your convenience.*
>
> *Thanks for your consideration,*
>
> *[Your Name]*
> *[Contact Info]*

19

Try different roads

You've got options.

No matter where you are in your job, it's natural to think about what's next. But "next" doesn't necessarily mean going somewhere else. It could mean trying another path at your current organization. After everything you've invested in your job, if you don't feel good about your fit, you owe it to yourself to explore other options.

So you did a baseline evaluation of job fit after acclimating to your new job in a new organization. That's smart. But the reality of your job and workplace tomorrow could be very different from what it is today. This means the dynamics of job fit are constantly in play. Maybe something big happens to you—say, you join a new team or department. Or change comes to your organization thanks to an acquisition, restructuring, a major policy change, or the introduction of a new line of business or leadership team.

After the dust settles on any of these events, take another look at how your job fit feels to you. These situations all represent opportunities to check in with yourself about what's working and what's not. You may choose to recalibrate your needs and expectations to take advantage of an exciting turn of events. Or you may find that you're bored, you've mastered your role, you want something new, or things feel way off, and you're thinking about moving on. This is understandable, but before you do that, investigate alternative paths within your organization that could strengthen your fit and advance your goals.

Exploring other options is well worth the effort before you make a major decision. Why? Before walking away, you want to ensure you get as much as possible from your circumstances, given the time and effort you've invested in your job. (Squeeze all the juice from the lemon!) If you discover there are no alternative paths that exist or appeal to you, you can be confident you've gotten everything you could from the job experience. Exploring all your options may lead you to an entirely different opportunity that you would have never considered or discovered if you bailed at the first hint of a fit problem.

Here are five options worth exploring to see if your fit is fixable:

Grow in place. One of the top ways to strengthen fit and increase job satisfaction is by growing skills and expertise. Tap your organization's resources to develop in your current role. Look for opportunities for training, certifications, continuing education, and mentorship. Solicit feedback from teammates and your manager so you can continue to improve, develop new skills, and apply your strengths. Ask for assignments that require you to stretch or to work on a high-profile project. You could say:

> *"I'm feeling confident in my current role and consistently meet my goals. I'm ready for additional challenges that will help me grow and contribute more to the team. I'm particularly interested in [specific type of project].*
>
> *I've been following [specific organizational initiative] and I am confident I could add value there. I'm committed to maintaining excellence in my current responsibilities while taking this on.*

Would you consider me for opportunities like this or help me identify what I need to be working on to be ready when the right stretch assignment comes up?"

Pursue a new or expanded role. When you offer to take on new responsibilities, it shows initiative, makes your organization's leaders more aware of you, and increases your chances for advancement. Identify areas where you can add value or where your skills have been overlooked. This could include tasks previously handled by someone else or tasks that are crucial to the business but have been underresourced. Proving yourself in a bigger role could result in a promotion and a new job title, too. Give your manager an updated job description or draft a new one entirely. (AI can help.) This will demonstrate your initiative and make it easier for your manager to advocate for you.

Make a lateral move. Explore opportunities to move to another team or a different department within your organization. Exposure to new functions or business units may give you a fresh perspective that's valuable to you and your employer. Learning new processes and applying your strengths in new ways could be energizing to you. A move to another part of the organization usually requires a high performance rating in your current role and an endorsement from your manager.

Get on the path to promotion. To earn a promotion, most organizations require consistently high performance for 18–36 months in a role before awarding a promotion. If you're unclear about promotion paths and criteria, ask your manager or HR what's required. With their support, map out an action plan with specific goals and a clear timeline.

Build a support system. A satisfying work experience takes support from colleagues you trust. Make a concerted effort to develop meaningful relationships with your coworkers. Offer your help to them and ask for their help. Get to know the interns, admins, and other staff who can provide insight or resources. Make friends on your team, in other departments, on other projects, and at different levels. Ask to manage a person or a team so you learn to delegate and help others grow. When you help others grow, they're more likely to support you in return. People remember who invested in their success and often become loyal allies.

It takes time to objectively evaluate your fit in a new role, team, or organization. It takes perspective to be able to evaluate it at various points in your career. You may be tempted to leave prematurely, but be aware of the potential unintended consequences later, when you might experience:

- Less fulfillment
- Less skill development
- Fewer mentorship opportunities
- Fewer chances to build leadership skills
- Loss of accumulated benefits
- Fewer professional references or job referrals
- Compensation ceilings when organizations value depth of experience

Your ego might try to convince you that a new job is the solution to all that's wrong and terrible in your current job. Don't be fooled. There's no guarantee a new job will be better until you're enlightened and skillful about how to address fit issues.

IRL

In her 20s, Shellye was a sought-after social media strategist and digital content creator. She was also a serial job hopper because her skills were in high demand, which enabled her to move up quickly and secure a six-figure salary before most of her friends. Despite this early success, she wasn't happy in any of her roles. She assumed that work would always be a grind and that she'd always have to keep looking for the next higher-paying gig.

When searching for her next opportunity, Shellye was surprised that the offers didn't pile up like they once did. Her therapist encouraged her to reflect on this and think about what made her leave previous roles behind. She acknowledged that she didn't have strong relationships with her colleagues and also felt insecure leading a team without having received leadership training.

This reflection led to an epiphany: Because she never stayed in any given role for more than a year, she never fully acclimated to a job or the organizations she worked for. She hadn't invested the time and effort to build relationships and had never taken advantage of professional development opportunities. She realized that her impact had been minimal because she never stuck around long enough to see projects through to the end.

Her only objective had been to move up quickly and make more money, but now she wanted something else. Rather than job hunting, she would make the most of the job she had. She decided to take a break from climbing the ladder to work on becoming a strong leader. She would devote her time to developing meaningful relationships with colleagues and take advantage of the leadership training programs offered by her employer. Shellye was determined to take responsibility for deepening her own job satisfaction this time around.

By thoroughly exploring all options within your organization, you ensure you've done everything possible to strengthen your fit. You're not only maximizing your investment today but also building the self-awareness and strategic thinking that will benefit you throughout your career. Whether you ultimately stay and succeed in a new role or leave for something else, you'll enjoy the peace of mind that comes from knowing you made an informed, intelligent choice. Sometimes the grass isn't greener on the other side—it's greener where you water it.

Think about it

Which of the five options for strengthening fit resonates most with you in your current circumstances?

Make a move

Take action on that option. Over the next 60–90 days, notice if fit feels stronger, weaker, or unchanged.

20

Know when to go

Move on with clarity and class.

What if you've done all you can to make your job a good fit for you, but it's just not happening? Or what if your goals or needs have changed? Maybe you're thinking about working part time or moving to another part of the country. Perhaps you've realized you don't want your boss's job and don't aspire to the lives of the leaders you're working for. Or you want to pivot to a new industry or just take a break.

Maybe you want to become a people manager, or the opposite—to stop managing people. Maybe you anticipate a large portion of your job will become automated soon due to the advancements of AI, so you want to be proactive. Maybe nothing has changed in your organization and you realize it never will.

No matter your reason, leaving your job doesn't have to be awkward or dramatic. It's commonplace. In fact, roughly 110,000 people quit their jobs daily in the US. And while baby boomers worked for approximately 6.6 employers from ages 25 to 52, Gen Zers are expected to end up working 18 jobs across six careers in their lifetime, according to the Bureau of Labor Statistics.

If you're crystal clear about your decision to move on—good for you. But what if despite trying different roads, and assessing all the dimensions of fit, you remain unsettled about your decision. How do you know when to go?

Listen to yourself. If you're still uncertain about when or if you will make a change, take the time to calmly and thoughtfully reflect on your values and needs. From a centered place, ask yourself, *What is the right next step?* Don't rush or force an answer, just listen. Are you ready for the change? Do you feel a sense of relief when you imagine making a certain decision?

You're still underpaid. You enjoy your work and the people you work with, but you know you're undercompensated. You've asked for a raise based on your market value and contributions to the organization, but your requests have been repeatedly rejected. Now you know you are not appropriately valued by your employer, so it's time to find a position elsewhere that reflects your worth.

There's no path. You want upward mobility, mentorship, and professional growth, but it's not available. You've been denied a promotion and other roles to explore. Your manager isn't championing you, and the organization isn't investing in you. If you can clearly account for how your job fit is unfixable, it's time to look for the next opportunity.

You've sought a second opinion. You talked with a mentor or two to get a seasoned and unbiased perspective. You described the situation and the options you've explored. Your mentors confirmed you haven't overlooked any paths available to you.

When you're ready to leave your job, it's always better to be moving toward something good than running away from something bad. This commonsense approach is not just better for your immediate financial security; hiring managers and recruiters favor employed candidates, and your negotiating position is often stronger when you have a job. Intentionally moving toward something good also makes it more likely you'll end up in a position that aligns with your strengths, values, and long-term aspirations. It also brings you closer to the dimensions of fit you've learned are most important to you, setting you up for future success and fulfillment, rather than merely escaping a negative situation.

Only you can decide what's best for you and when to go. Once you do, it's *how* you leave that matters most. People remember departures, and how you handle yours will reflect on your professional reputation for years to come, so don't burn bridges. Be in a rational, calm state of mind when you share your news to leave. Resist crying and avoid blaming anyone, and don't allow yourself to be drawn into unproductive or emotionally charged conversations.

Wrap up loose ends on current projects, and work with your manager and HR on timing, communication, and transition plans. Be sure to thank them for the opportunity and share something positive you learned from the experience. Send handwritten notes to colleagues you worked closely with. Be upbeat and appreciative as you depart, and share your personal contact information to stay in touch.

IRL

Diana worked for an up-and-coming consumer brand. She felt proud to be associated with a cool company that impressed her friends. But the culture was oppressive.

There was little collaboration or interest in her point of view. She was silenced in meetings by domineering leaders. Directives were given by leadership, and everyone was expected to execute without asking questions or contributing to the solutions. Diana worked until late in the evenings and most weekends and was given no interns or junior associates to support her. Even though she had 10 years of experience and expertise to bring to the team, she struggled to feel good about her fit.

She carefully evaluated her options, but the company was too small for her to move to another department, and her request for training was turned down. Diana had expected support and mentorship from the female leaders, but they, too, were overworked, overwhelmed, and underappreciated. She realized it was time to go and seek a role in a bigger company that was more compatible with her working style and values.

No job is meant to last forever. Each job serves a purpose for you during a particular time. That could be financial security, professional growth, camaraderie, or convenience. When you've done all your homework and you're clear about your needs and objectives, the decision may feel easy and even liberating.

If it's not a fit, move on. You deserve better.

Think about it 

What signs are telling you it's time to go? What signs, if any, are telling you to stay?

Make a move 

If it's possible to strengthen fit, commit to staying and working to improve fit. If it's not, make a plan and commit to leaving with class.

PART 3
WRAP UP

The workplace will always be evolving, but the fundamentals of fit are constant: alignment between you, your role, your environment, and the organization. These aren't luxuries—they're essentials for a fulfilling career and reaching your potential. Understanding and applying the Work Fit Framework will serve you in any economy, any industry, and at any stage of your career. Don't wait for the stars to align or for someone else to hand you the ideal job. Take charge, make informed decisions, and create the career you want. The tools are in your hands now.

- **Size things up** to understand and evaluate all the dimensions of fit in your job.
- **Know your value** to determine if you are fairly compensated.
- **Make your work matter** to unlock your intrinsic motivation.
- **Land a great boss** who will invest in your growth and champion your success.
- **Try different roads** to proactively strengthen fit in your current role.
- **Know when to go** to take the next step with confidence.

Go at your own speed

Careers are no longer linear. Or static. Or monolithic. (That era is over.) Careers are dynamic, diverse, and individualized. They go up, down, and sideways. Careers pivot, pause, and restart. Sometimes you hit a moment in your career where you need to think about what's next. That's why it may be more useful to think of your career in terms of shapes rather than paths.

Career shapes are based on your choices, experiences, and aspirations. Career shapes include an overall trajectory that has twists and turns, enriching experiments, and opportunities for growth.

As your career unfolds, you can choose to shape it based on your life stage or circumstances. You'll discover that your pace will change to meet your needs (so play the long game). Sometimes you'll want to slow down. Sometimes you'll want to accelerate—to learn more, do more, or earn more. Or you may want to take a break or go in a new direction.

It's *up* to you.

Career Shape	Description
1. **The Chill** 	You hold one role that stays relatively unchanged over time.
2. **The Slow Roll** 	You hold a role in one discipline that evolves gradually.
3. **The Hike** 	You focus intensely on skill-building and upward momentum.
4. **The Zig Zag** 	You explore different fields and roles at an unpredictable pace.
5. **The Lattice** 	You pursue multiple disciplines to broaden your skill set and accelerate later.
6. **The Jolt** 	You advance quickly early on, then plateau with deep expertise.
7. **The Gaps** 	You pursue single or multiple disciplines with intentional breaks aligned with life needs.
8. **The Portfolio** 	You manage a variety of roles based on expertise and interest.
9. **The Hustle** 	You work one primary role with multiple side gigs, sometimes leading to growth.
10. **The Spiral** 	You pursue entrepreneurship for freedom and independence, working at an intense pace.

Explore the shapes. Based on coaching thousands of individuals, Equipt Women observed common themes emerging from various career choices and outcomes. Themes emerged that were synthesized into ten distinct shapes.

Assess and pursue yours. Consider what shape best reflects how your career has unfolded so far. Is that the shape you intended for your career? Or is there another shape that looks more inspiring and is a better fit? Choose a shape that works for you or create your own without apology or regret. You may choose one shape now and a different shape in the future. Recognize that you will experience different career phases or have different careers altogether, so your shape will change over time.

Make sure the shape of your career delights and satisfies you. If it doesn't, reshape it!

Part 4

THINK BIG(GER)

'FESS UP REST UP

UP SKILL UP POWER

POWER UP STAND U

UP RAMP UP GEAR

P PUMP UP 'FESS UP

UP OPEN UP RISE

P STEP UP LIFT UP

MOVE UP FIRE UP S

SHOW UP LEVEL UP

ST SPEAK UP MOVE

'FESS UP REST UP S

UP SKILL UP POWER

POWER UP STAND U

Do you ever wonder what happened to the big, exciting future you envisioned for your life when you were a kid? Everything seemed possible. Your dreams felt within reach. "You can be anything you want," was the mantra from supportive teachers and parents. But your world started shrinking as your mind filled up with the tasks and obligations that come with "adulting." Pay your bills. Finish that assignment for your boss. Get groceries for the week. And remember to have fun, too. Reality can be a drag, making you and your life feel small and uninspiring. How are you supposed to pursue your dreams when your days are consumed by a daily to-do list?

You learn to think bigger.

Thinking bigger redirects your attention from what's in front of you right now to what's possible in the future. By intentionally clearing away the small stuff that eats up your time and energy, you create space for fresh, expansive thinking that opens up a rich landscape of opportunity. For example:

> When you think small, you fixate on getting a raise. When you think big, you imagine how you might run the organization one day.
>
> When you think small, you leave a comment about someone else's content. When you think big, you're hatching an idea for a killer podcast of your own.
>
> When you think small, you take on a freelance gig to make some extra cash. When you think big, you're strategizing how to turn your side hustle into a successful start-up.

As your mind shifts from small thinking to big thinking, you start to feel eager to see more, feel more, and do more. You seek out bold ideas and intriguing challenges. You pursue your ambition without hesitation or needing other people's approval. You may feel some trepidation, but you push through anyway. Nothing holds you back.

It may be hard to shake off the setbacks or self-doubt or fear that have kept you idling in place for so long. Maybe you feel safe within the routines you've created for yourself. Maybe you're overwhelmed by too much work or other responsibilities in your life. Or maybe you think chasing a bigger life than the one you have is audacious—*How could that even be possible?* Or immodest—*I'm not ready!* Or impractical—*There's too much competition!*

There's nothing wrong with wanting more. You ought to want more, because you deserve more. And thinking bigger is your ticket to the land of more. More personal growth, more joy, more opportunity. More options and more freedom.

Thinking bigger begins with making space in your life for discovery.

This space enables you to embark on a treasure hunt for gems of inspiration and insight that strengthen your sense of self and expand your perception of what's possible. Eventually, you'll stop thinking about the pin on the map that shows where you are, and you'll start seeing the multitude of paths that can take you anywhere you want to go.

In my 20s, I worked at an industrial design firm with a talented team of engineers, designers, and marketing professionals who taught me a ton about thinking bigger. The firm had a reputation as a design think tank, a kind of Big Idea factory that attracted Fortune 500 clients. The secret to the team's creative success came down to three simple questions that never failed to provoke major breakthroughs. The first two were "Why?" and "Why not?"

The team used the question "Why?" to understand the status quo. Being exploratory rather than confrontational helped us deeply probe a problem and better understand a user's needs. Asked multiple times until it could no longer be answered, "Why?" was like a tool for excavating original insights that would eventually lead to a solution. For example, when working on a project for a major consumer goods company, we asked a focus group of campers:

- Why do you enjoy camping? (A. Because it's fun.)
- Why is it fun? (A. Because I get to spend time in nature.)
- Why is spending time in nature important? (A. Because it's peaceful.)

- Why is it peaceful? (A. Because it helps me disconnect from work.)
- Why is disconnecting important? (A. Because I need work-life balance.)
- Why is work-life balance important? (A. Because I need to chill; I need peace.)

Then we used the question "Why not?" to challenge our understanding of the status quo. "Why not?" had an energetic, optimistic vibe that suggested there were no insurmountable obstacles. It encouraged us to challenge norms and imagine futures that didn't exist . . . yet. For example:

- Why not create the most peaceful camping experience?
- Why not make disconnecting easy, enjoyable, and rejuvenating?
- Why not encourage camping as the ideal way to disconnect?
- Why not make it convenient for people to spend more time in nature?

"Why?" and "Why not?" were simple tools to get people thinking beyond the obvious and prevented premature or nearsighted conclusions. Then a final question expanded the realm of possibility further: "What if?"

- What if sleeping was no longer necessary?
- What if campgrounds were more appealing than hotels?
- What if disconnecting happened automatically?
- What if everyone was a camper?
- What if the benefits of being in nature could be woven into everyday life?

Working in such a curious-minded culture for almost a decade took some getting used to. But as this approach became a regular practice for me, my ideas got bigger, and so did my career and life.

Thinking bigger doesn't require working in a creative environment or natural talent. On the contrary, it's a vital skill anyone can develop. Thinking bigger is a courageous, purposeful act, an exhilarating declaration that you embrace a world of possibilities.

When you're free from self-imposed limitations, you can paint your life in bold, confident strokes. Sure, you'll still have daily responsibilities, but you'll tackle them with renewed energy and optimism, inspired by the vast horizon ahead.

Think bigger, and every action you take will move you *up.*

21

Nix the negatives

Make room for bigger and better.

Have you ever felt stressed when getting dressed for a big meeting at work because you can't decide what to wear? Your closet is full of clothes, and you know there's a great outfit hiding in there somewhere, but it's hard to find because it's buried among all the clothes you don't wear anymore. The old things are taking up valuable space in your closet.

The same is true in life. The useless, negative stuff in your life occupies valuable space in your head and suffocates your vibe. Negative influences will try to crowd you from every direction. When left unmanaged, they become reflections of your environment, the people around you, and your thoughts. They drain your time, energy, and focus, leaving you with little left to invest in yourself.

In the personal coaching world, negative influences are called "tolerations." Consciously or unconsciously, you put up with many of them daily. Some are big—an unsupportive boss or an unhealthy romantic relationship. Some are small(er)—irritating coworkers or unfinished projects around the house that nag at you. When you're aware of your tolerations, you can address them head on. Here's how:

Take inventory. Over the course of a week, take two minutes after dinner each day to identify the tolerations in your routine, environment, or relationships that may be bogging you down. After a week, review your inventory and determine which items are taking the most attention and energy from you. Your list may be short or long. There is no magic number. Then decide what you will eliminate, what you will improve, and what you will let go.

Eliminate it. These are the things you have the power to change by removing the problem. Turn off notifications and alerts that interrupt your train of thought. Unfollow people on social media who provoke you or cause anxiety. Stop spending time with unsupportive friends or gossipy colleagues. Unsubscribe from newsletters that swamp your inbox. Call a plumber to stop the leaky faucet that's keeping you up at night. RSVP no to the party you've been dreading.

Improve it. These are the things you have the power to change by making the situation better. Place time limits on tasks that get on your nerves. Disengage with the office gossip by saying, *"I have had a positive experience with that person"* or *"I'd rather not discuss this."* Pay a little extra to park closer to your office so you aren't stressed about getting to work on time. Get noise-canceling headphones to drown out the loud music blaring at the gym. Have an honest conversation with your roommate or partner about fairly dividing household chores.

Let it go. These are things you can't eliminate or improve (or choose not to), so you commit to not being bothered by them. No more complaining or allowing these things to suck your finite energy. Another organizational shake-up is happening; it's out of your control. Your ex is getting married; let it go. Smile and keep talking when people arrive late to your big speech. Ignore a friend's flippant comment about your new outfit.

Shake it off when a blind date goes sideways. Make the bed in the morning when your partner forgets to do it.

Make a plan. After you've decided whether you're going to eliminate, improve, or let go of your tolerations, create a strategy for making that happen. Prioritize based on your work style. If you're the kind of person who needs to move the boulder out of the way first, start with the big tolerations that are taking the most attention and energy from you. If you're usually motivated by a few easy wins, tackle the small stuff first. Just don't try to do it all at once. Tick them off one by one until you've got them under control. And note that some tolerations—such as an overly chatty colleague—may be difficult to eliminate, so you might have to switch to an improve or let-it-go approach along the way.

IRL

Aja was excited to reconnect with three of her college roommates when they all moved to the same city several years after graduation. Her enthusiasm to relive those collegiate years and the need to share living expenses motivated her to move in with her friends.

Her enthusiasm was short-lived. She quickly discovered that despite having full-time jobs, the roommates hadn't matured since college. They partied excessively night after night. They left food containers on the coffee table and dirty dishes piled high in the sink. Their friends, who frequently dropped by, often spent the night without paying for the groceries they consumed or contributing to the rent.

The situation at home was taking a toll on Aja. She felt tired all the time and was so stressed and grumpy that she stopped going to the gym after work. Instead, she went home and locked herself in her room to avoid interacting with the roommates and dealing with the mess in the kitchen. She realized she had outgrown her college friends, who were oblivious to their impact on her well-being despite Aja's attempts to discuss her concerns with them.

Aja knew she had to move on, even if it meant losing these friends forever. She found someone to sublet her room and then rented a tiny studio she could afford on her own. Within weeks, she felt like herself again—upbeat, energetic, and self-assured. This new sense of physical and mental space brought positive momentum back to Aja's life.

When you spend your energy on things that eat away at you and wear you down, there's no gas left in the tank to drive yourself forward. That's why addressing the tolerations in your life is essential for making way for the bigger life you want. This ongoing personal housekeeping will ensure you have the time and energy you need to invest in your future.

Think about it 

What tolerations in your life are taking the most time and energy from you?

Make a move 

Choose one toleration and take steps to eliminate it, improve it, or let it go.

22

Care more about less

Lighten your load.

It's easy to get caught up in a whirlwind of activity around you, only to realize that you've become absorbed in a lot of little things that don't really matter to you. Maybe it's your neighbor's seemingly endless vacation posts on social media. Or you were the only one who couldn't make it to book club (again). Or maybe you can't stop noticing how your college roommate was promoted (again). These kinds of things sort of sneak into your brain, and before you know it, they're gobbling up your valuable headspace. You might also be oblivious when one of them hijacks your brain entirely, stealing the oxygen from everything else you need to be focused on.

This situation may sound dire, but the solution is simple: Care more about less.

When you care more about less, you choose to focus on a small set of your key priorities and sideline everything else. Devoting your energy to what you care about most enables you to spend your resources on the parts of your life that provide the greatest return on your investment.

When you care more about less, you align your mental, emotional, and intellectual energy to make clear-headed choices about what matters to you. If you pay attention to the inconsequential stuff, it's hard to see your values reflected in what you do every day. Your critical thinking breaks down, and you make irrational decisions that lead to places you really don't want to end up. Put simply, you squander your valuable finite energy.

Here's a practical insight about energy: Energy follows attention. And what you pay attention to grows bigger. Think about when you have a tiny pimple on your face. You keep checking it in the mirror, and it seems like a massive thing that everyone *must* be staring at. Some people may notice it, while others may not notice it at all. But it's a big deal to you because you're fixated on it. That's how your attention works—whatever we focus on becomes bigger. This energy-attention principle also applies to positive outcomes. For instance, if you practice noticing three things you're grateful for each day, your sense of gratitude will expand because you purposely direct your attention there.

Use this approach to care more about less and focus your attention on what matters most to you.

Prioritize. What do you care about the most? Maybe it's getting that overdue promotion, buying a car, paying off college debt, saving for a home, moving to another city, adopting a pet, finding a new job, raising a happy child, having a few close friends, or getting in shape. Try to name your top three priorities. If you're unsure what they are, reflect on your values to get started. For instance, if one of your values is community, how much time each week are you dedicating to nurturing your current community or creating a new one? If the answer is very little or none, you may want to prioritize attending an event with friends, inviting a coworker to lunch, or spending time with family.

Remind yourself. Put your priorities right in front of you so that they can influence your conscious and unconscious thoughts and decision-making. Write them down using whatever works best for you—your notes app, a recurring event on your calendar, a journal, a screensaver, or Post-it notes on your laptop. This will remind you at the start of each day what really matters to you.

Manage your time. Does your calendar show that you're spending enough time on what matters most to you? Are you allocating time each day, week, month, or quarter to these things? Assign a color to priority activities so you can see at a glance how your time spent aligns with your priorities. It will also make it easy to eliminate or minimize time spent on activities that don't align with your priorities.

Choose fewer things. If you reduce the number of things you're focused on, you can give those fewer things the attention they deserve. Instead of being involved with three community organizations, pick one. Instead of trying to become highly competent at every aspect of your role, master one skill at a time. For example, become great at data visualization rather than spreading yourself thin across research, analysis, and presentation design. Or choose quality over quantity with your projects. Deliberately take on fewer initiatives so you can deliver exceptional, impactful work.

Apply this to your personal life, too. If your friends are planning a weekend getaway, and it's not in your budget because you're prioritizing paying off college debt or saving for grad school, tell them, *"It sounds fun. I can't make it work this time. Have a great time!"*

Be open with your manager, select coworkers, family, and close friends by sharing what matters most to you. Let them know you're making necessary choices about how to spend your time, money, and energy.

Keep your eye on the ball. When you're tempted to give your attention to unimportant things, don't. Acknowledge these distractions, then let them go. They will always come at you fast and furious, so practice redirecting your attention to what matters most to you. If you find yourself stressing about what someone thinks of you, note the thought and remind yourself that their opinions are not within your control.

What if, despite your best efforts, your mind keeps dwelling on something you deemed a low priority? Consider that it might be more important to you than you realize!

IRL

Carrie has a lot going on: a demanding job, a 30-minute commute, business travel, one kid in kindergarten, and the other a middle-schooler who plays multiple sports. She often rushes through the drop-off line at school, arrives late to soccer games, and is rarely able to volunteer at the concession stand.

Because she was always in a hurry, Carrie never had time to chat or make friends with other parents. Even though she did what she could by contributing money to support after-school activities, she was not a part of the sports and other social circles in her small town.

Standing alone on the sidelines at the soccer field, Carrie often found herself ruminating about what an outsider she felt herself to be. One day, she realized that instead of having fun watching her kid pretend he's Lionel Messi, she was brooding again over how unpopular she must be with the other kids' parents.

That wasn't normally a thought that would even occur to her. But now, it was all she could think about when she attended school or sports events. When her mind started racing, she noted she was obsessing again—physically present, but mentally absent—and missing her kid's game! Then she reminded herself that she had two great kids and a job she loved, which were her top priorities. Worrying about what the other parents were thinking was siphoning precious mental energy away from the things she cared about most.

The next day, Carrie gave a friendly wave to the other parents as she dropped her kids at school. Later, she gave a kick-ass presentation to her company's executive leadership, then headed to her son's soccer game, where she cheered from the stands like a superfan. After the game, she took her kids for pizza and laughed at the goofy stories they told her about their day. She was happy to discover how relaxed she felt at the end of a busy day. It was as if she'd found an extra hour in her pocket to spend on what mattered most. Ka-ching!

When you devote more time and energy to what's meaningful to you and less to what's trivial, you'll have the emotional and intellectual bandwidth to invest in new ideas and bigger possibilities. You'll be able to think strategically about your future, nurture cherished relationships, and do your best work on what counts. It's the difference between spinning your wheels and gaining real momentum.

Who or what is taking up excessive time and energy in your life that isn't truly important to you?

Make a move

Focus on the one thing that matters most to you right now. Devote 10 percent more of your time and energy to it this week and 20 percent less on the person or thing that isn't important to you.

23

Expand your worldview

See life through a bigger lens.

Routines are comforting. They bring structure and stability to daily life and reduce decision fatigue. That's why so many famous tech leaders resort to a simple uniform of a T-shirt and jeans, so they can spend their time inventing the "Next Big Thing" rather than thinking about what to wear every day. You probably have routines, too. Make your bed daily, go to the same coffee shop every morning, eat dinner at a designated time, or stretch before going to bed. We all need some routines.

Yet too many routines keep your world small. You find yourself idling in place rather than exploring what life has to offer. Routines create a bubble around you that keeps you from experiencing spontaneous connections or adventures. Too many routines can stifle creativity and growth. They can also lead to tunnel vision. A life that's overly rooted in routine prevents you from discovering the kindling needed to spark bigger thinking.

The best way to break out of your routine rut is to make your world bigger.

The world gets bigger when you see more of it. Expanding your worldview—the way you see or perceive the world—takes you beyond your own behavior patterns, beliefs, and experiences to discover what's outside of your immediate sightline. Every step you take in this larger world stretches you and puts your mind in a place it's never been before. This intellectual and creative journey reduces your blind spots and frees you to see things previously invisible to you. You might even experience a sense of wonder and more empathy.

Here's how to see the world through a bigger lens:

Diversify your info diet. Consume a range of media that spans ideologies, geographies, and subject matters. Engage with people whose backgrounds and experience are different from yours. Study aspects of history you're unfamiliar with to understand what came before you.

Get out of your bubble. Travel to new places, immerse yourself in the culture, and connect with the locals. If it's not possible to travel, you can get a taste of all that (without even cracking your passport) by learning a language, watching movies from across the globe, or trying different ethnic cuisines. Just venturing beyond your own neighborhood changes your perspective. The whole world is out there—go experience it.

Question your assumptions. Before you decide how or why something is the way it is, ask yourself what assumptions you have about it. You may have biases or preconceived ideas that prevent you from seeing the whole picture. For example, if you're interested in a role and you don't have 100 percent of the qualifications, you might assume it's not worth applying. When in fact, if you have 60–80 percent of the qualifications, you're most likely a viable candidate. Then ask yourself whether there are other perspectives to consider. (Spoiler alert: The answer will always be yes.) How does someone else's perspective change yours? Are your assumptions helping you or holding you back?

IRL

Zahra worked for a New York–based brand consulting firm. After months of preparation, she gave a presentation to a major Midwestern window manufacturing company on how to increase the appeal of their products to architects and designers. But the audience of senior engineers stared blankly after she finished her presentation. There were no smiles, nods, or applause. Dejected and confused, she had no idea what went wrong.

After the meeting, an executive who had attended the presentation pulled her aside to offer some friendly feedback: "You sound like a cardiologist explaining a bypass procedure." At first, she didn't follow. Then he explained that she had been speaking a "design" language that didn't make sense to her nondesigner audience.

She realized she had based her entire presentation on what she assumed the client needed and neglected to spend time with them to learn firsthand about their products and their customers' pain points. To rectify the situation, she asked if she could spend a week at the company's headquarters to join product meetings, talk to workers in the factory, and lead a customer focus group. Her goal was to listen and learn. This enabled her to tune in to their culture and the vocabulary they used to talk about their business. This helped her to better relate to their needs and brainstorm solutions to their problems that she hadn't previously considered.

Weeks later, Zahra made a presentation to the same audience and was acknowledged with a roaring round of applause.

Exploring a larger world will reveal unexpected connections and patterns that challenge your long-held beliefs and your sense of what's possible. You may begin to feel more comfortable navigating ambiguity and complexity. You may also feel slightly nervous or uncomfortable as you broaden your horizons and explore new concepts. Don't worry, this is just the growing pains for your expanding worldview, paving the way for your big ideas.

Think about it

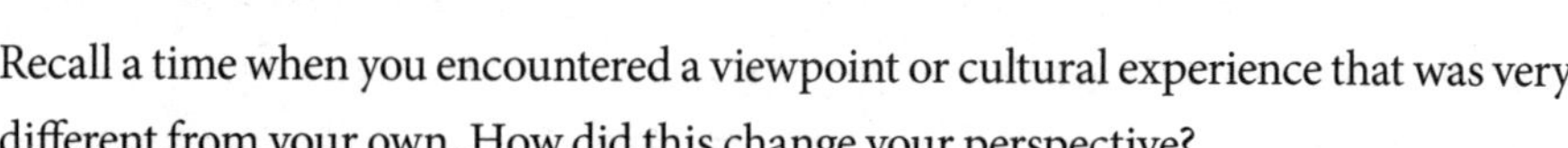

Recall a time when you encountered a viewpoint or cultural experience that was very different from your own. How did this change your perspective?

Make a move 

Explore one way to actively expand your worldview. For example, ask to join a cross-functional project at work to gain exposure to different teams. Or go to a play that's performed in a different language from your own.

24

Find inspiration

When you feel the spark, you know it.

Inspiration is that spark of energy and excitement you experience that may be triggered by anything at all. A moving story, the color of the sunset, a line from a song, or a beat of stillness. This spark may cause a fleeting flicker of curiosity and delight, or it may propel you to go out and do something big. In that moment, the spark of inspiration actually changes you.

When you're inspired, you see and experience the world in a different light. Suddenly, there are more possibilities in front of you. The doubts or excuses that usually hold you back fade and then disappear. You feel a rush of energy that compels you to act.

You can't force inspiration to strike, but you can cultivate it, like a flower garden. A garden needs the right conditions to thrive—good soil, sunlight, and water. Inspiration happens under the right conditions, too. When you have an open and relaxed mind and abundant stimulation, the sparks of inspiration fly.

To put yourself in situations where inspiration can find you:

Engage with art. Visit museums, galleries, craft fairs, car shows, live theater, and concerts. Linger with pieces you're drawn to. Look for the emotion in what you see. Find out more about the creator. If art isn't your thing, listen to music from a wide variety of genres. How does the music make you feel?

Study people. Learn about the visionaries, pioneers, and leaders driven to make change, innovate, or make the world a better place. Understand what makes them tick and how they spend their time. Talk to people you admire who genuinely enjoy their work about what factors contribute to their fulfillment. What attributes do the people you're interested in have in common?

Study organizations that resonate with you. What organizations or brands are you consistently attracted to? Understand the strategies that make them successful, how they make people feel, and what problems they solve. Explore their business models and how and where they operate. Identify brands that appeal to your values and emotions. Notice products that make you wonder, *How did they do that?*

Spend time in nature. Put your devices away and walk distraction-free in a botanical garden or on a nature path around your neighborhood. Spend time in wide-open spaces, such as parks or along the shoreline. Engage your senses. Touch grass. Smell the air. Taste fresh herbs. Listen to birds communicate. Sit on a bench and watch squirrels do what squirrels do. What do you see that you haven't noticed before?

Look back. Root through old photographs and childhood artifacts to uncover clues you left behind. Talk to family or friends about what they remember about your fascinations back then. You might find that you're reminded of a part of yourself that you unknowingly or reluctantly left behind, or perhaps had forgotten about, which could inspire you now.

Reflect. Inspiration often comes not in the moment but in the space between experiences, when your mind makes unexpected connections. Create quiet time to let your mind wander and then settle. In stillness, your imagination often makes magic from what's inspired you.

IRL

Monique had a good job in finance, but she was bored and uninspired. She chose her profession at her father's encouragement because it was prestigious, well paying, and offered upward mobility. However, she found her work uninspiring and she couldn't imagine doing it much longer. She didn't have interests or hobbies outside of work, and most weekends were spent moping around her apartment. She dreaded Mondays and didn't much look forward to Fridays either.

With the help of a friend eager to see Monique be happier, she decided to rewire her weekends. Instead of hanging around her apartment, she set out to explore the city with a fresh mind. She started dropping in at new breakfast spots, taking trips to the farmers market, and peeking inside bookstores and galleries. After taking a walk along the river, she'd prepare a simple, home-cooked dinner. After a few weekends spent this way, Monique felt something light up inside her. She was enjoying smells she had never noticed before. She appreciated the presentation of fresh vegetables that she didn't always see in her neighborhood grocery store. She taught herself new recipes. She felt healthy and more alive than she had in years.

Soon, she was considering possibilities she had never contemplated. She realized that health and wellness—not finance—were exciting to her. She began looking for job opportunities at health-focused companies and even started to explore getting a master's in health and wellness management. A vivid spark of inspiration led Monique to her next chapter.

The beautiful thing about inspiration is that it's everywhere, waiting to be discovered. You don't need to travel to exotic places or have extraordinary experiences—you just need to open your eyes to what's already around you. And when inspiration strikes, look out! You tingle with excitement to act on whatever ignited you. Seize that feeling and keep going. Generate bigger and better ideas and possibilities so you live your life in full bloom.

Think about it 

Recall a time when you felt inspired by something or someone new to you? What happened as a result of that experience?

Make a move 

Dedicate one Saturday each month to cultivating inspiration in your life.

25

Picture your future

When you can see it,
it's easier to create it.

When you imagine your future, what do you see?

For many people, the picture is fuzzy. That's because we don't often make a deliberate effort to think beyond the next paycheck, promotion, or vacation. Or we might dream about the distant future, but don't have a way to harness those thoughts and make them concrete and useful.

Imagining your future is a powerful form of visualization that can crystallize what you want and what you're working toward. This clarity makes you feel more in control of your life's direction. When you vividly imagine your future, you make more deliberate choices that will take you there.

When you think about where you want to be in your career and life five or ten years from now, the goal isn't to imagine a perfect future but rather one that excites and motivates you. Instead of limiting your picture of the future to what seems achievable right now, be boldly aspirational. Explore new ideas and possibilities that feel out of reach. When you picture your future, ask yourself, *What does a great day in my ideal future look like? What am I doing, who am I with, and how do I feel?* The answers to these questions can unlock powerful (and empowering) possibilities.

Here's how to bring your future into focus:

Visualize your vision. Pick a date two to five years in the future and imagine what you are doing for a living, what your schedule is like, what you do evenings and weekends, where you're living, who is in your life, and what your lifestyle is like. Gather images, words, and phrases from magazines, newspapers, or apps like Canva or Pinterest that capture some aspect of these details. Create a collage from this material and place it where you'll see it often—near your desk, in your bedroom, or on the fridge—to remind you what you're working toward. Continue adding to this collage, and don't worry if you're not sure how it all fits together. It's not a fixed image of your future; it's an evolving reflection of your vision as it takes shape.

For a more immersive experience, try using AI video tools to create short clips of yourself as an avatar living aspects of your ideal future (giving that keynote speech, working in your dream office, or celebrating a major milestone). These personal "life trailers" may help you visualize not just what you want, but how it might feel to live it.

Find a powerful object. Look for a meaningful item that symbolizes something specific you aspire to—a new experience, career, or quality you hope to embody. The object might be anything—a piece of art or jewelry, or a book. When you hold this item or look at it, let it remind you of the future you are creating.

Write a letter from your future. Imagine yourself five years from now and draft a message to who you are today. What would you want to say? Describe the choices you're grateful to have made, the risks you've taken, the people who have supported you, and the wisdom you've gleaned. This creates a greater awareness of what you can do today to move toward the future you want tomorrow.

Add a zero. Are you thinking big enough? Most people don't. Write down how much money you want to be making in 10 years. Now add a zero. How does that feel? Or if you read three books last year, imagine a future where you're reading 30 books a year. Or envision a future where your network has grown by 10x. See your future in the biggest terms possible.

Make a date with the future. Set aside time twice a year for a meeting with yourself (yes, just you). Think of it as your prearranged reality check. Assess if you are moving toward or away from your desired future. Where are you making progress, big or small? What are your barriers to progressing? Is the future you envisioned still exciting to you? Or do you want to make some tweaks to your vision of the future? If so, go for it!

IRL

Claudia is a single mother of teenage boys. She was a teen herself when she had both kids and managed to raise them with little support from their father or her family. She was the family breadwinner from a young age, so she needed a stable job to provide for her kids. She became a hairstylist, which allowed her to make ends meet by building a clientele of appreciative customers.

When she was 34, a pilot friend offered to take Claudia for a ride in their private plane. It was exhilarating for her to sit in the copilot's seat with a full view of the ocean to her right and the mountains to her left. She was mesmerized by the dashboard and wondered what each of the levers and dials controlled.

When they landed, the pilot said, "You loved this so much. Think about becoming a pilot yourself." Claudia laughed, thinking, *Sure, that'd be great, but I've got kids; I've got responsibilities!* But the more she thought about it, she realized she'd dreamed of becoming a pilot since the first time she'd flown on a plane a decade earlier. Suddenly, something clicked in her. Why not become a pilot? She could see herself in the pilot's seat. The mere thought of it made her heart race.

Later that same week, she spotted a toy plane on the ground near her car in a parking lot. She picked it up and took it home. For months, the plane sat on her coffee table. She couldn't stop staring at it. She started picturing a future where she had earned her pilot's license. It was thrilling to imagine. She began researching the certification process for pilots, the cost and time commitment, and grants that might be available to help fund this journey. Every time she held that little plane in her hand, she felt more determined to turn this dream into her new reality.

When you have a vision of your future, it keeps your aspirations right in front of you. It becomes a North Star that guides you toward opportunities you might have otherwise deemed unrealistic. Another way to think about it is this: When you can see your future, you can make your future.

Think about it 

Close your eyes and draw a mental picture of your future. Where do you see yourself in one year? Five years? Ten years? What will you be proud of? What will give you a sense of fulfillment?

Make a move 

Declare one thing you want in your future that seems out of reach. Visualize it with words, images, and objects.

26

Take aim

Pick a direction and test it out.

You don't need to be in your 40s and experiencing a midlife crisis to wonder if you're on the right path. Many people, regardless of age, sometimes feel like they ought to be somewhere else, doing something else with someone else. Maybe you do too, but you can't picture what that something is. That lack of certainty is why so many people choose to stay put or accept the status quo as inevitable. It feels safer to go nowhere than to go somewhere they're unsure of.

Here's the thing: You don't need to know your final destination to make a change in your life. Instead, take aim at a spot in the distance and start moving in that direction, one small step at a time.

Taking aim removes the pressure to "have it all figured out" before you take action. When you're not fixated on a specific destination, you're free to explore different facets of your future vision and test different paths that might get you there. You take low-risk, incremental steps that will tell you whether the direction you're headed is worth exploring further. If so, keep going. If not, regroup and adjust your aim. Either way, you're getting exactly the answers you're looking for without investing too much time or other resources.

For example, maybe you've been thinking about getting an MBA. Knowing it'll cost you big bucks and time away from the career path you've been on, you'd like to be sure an MBA is what you really want. Instead of plunging into GMAT prep and applying to a bunch of business schools, you take a few months to test the idea of going to grad school. How? You could take an online business course. You could read a stack of seminal books on management. You could have coffee with different people who've gotten their MBA to hear about their experience. You could ask your boss for a stretch assignment that will expose you to other business functions in your organization.

Then what?

If you're energized by any or all of those small steps, keep going. You could seek out a conversation with one or more of your organization's senior leaders. With this exposure, you might inquire about how their MBA is applied daily and the overall career benefits they've encountered. These types of conversations could help you discover possible paths an MBA might lead to, such as corporate strategy and business development, operations management, or business intelligence. Taking aim in the direction of an MBA can give you a much clearer picture of what you might want to be doing in the future.

Taking aim encourages you to step out into the world to discover where it's possible to go. You'll encounter various paths, lively detours, and unexpected insights. All of these experiences will sharpen your vision of your future. Think of it as test-driving your potential future. Here's how:

Pick a direction. Identify something about the future you've envisioned. This might be working in a new industry, moving into a different role, earning an advanced degree, or starting a family. Or it could be living in another part of the world, pursuing a different lifestyle, or making a specific form of impact.

Take small steps. Map out the smallest possible low-risk steps that allow you to "taste test" as you move in the direction you're exploring. Add steps or adjust your path as you learn from each experience. Get feedback from mentors, friends, or trusted colleagues. Here are some examples of the kinds of small steps you might take:

If your aim is to work in a new industry, you could:

- Reach out to people working in that industry and interview them about their journey.
- Attend a relevant industry conference or meetup.
- Research the best organizations to work for in that industry.

If your aim is a new role, you could:

- Shadow someone for a day or more in that role.
- Interview someone in the role about what they enjoy and don't.
- Create a related side hustle to see if the work excites you.

If your aim is to start a family, you could:

- Talk to other people who have done it alone or with a partner.
- Research your organization's policies for health care and parental leave.
- Explore your pathways (conception, fertility treatments, adoption, fostering, and surrogacy). Develop a budget for what may be required for your potential path.

If your aim is to live and work in a different part of the world, you could:

- Take a vacation there first.

- Talk to people who have made a similar move.
- Seek out an opportunity to live there for a short period (less than 90 days, no visa is needed).

IRL

Born and raised in the United States, Pauline always wanted to live and work in a part of the world where she could improve her Spanish. She couldn't afford to just pick up and move there without a job, and she didn't want to sell everything and change her life so drastically without more certainty about her decision.

Instead, she patiently explored open positions online for remote roles. This would allow her to inch in the direction of moving to Central or South America without making a risky leap. Eventually, she landed a client management job with a large business services company. The job was primarily conducted by email, Zoom and phone, so her physical presence was not required by the clients or the company.

After one year of high performance, she asked her manager if she could work from another country. They supported her request, as long as she remained on the company's West Coast time zone hours. This allowed her to sublet her apartment and take short-term rentals in different locations, including Mexico City, Panama, and Colombia. Having the flexibility to experience another part of the world and do her job was a great way to assess whether she'd really want to make a more permanent move one day—which she did!

Taking aim is a low-risk, low-pressure way to think bigger without making big commitments. Each small step reveals what energizes you and what doesn't, giving you the information you need to keep going or change direction. You don't need all the answers before you begin; you just need to select a direction that appeals to you and start moving. Then let the path reveal itself. By taking aim, you can explore a life before it becomes your life—the life truly meant for you.

What direction have you always wanted to explore but haven't yet?

Take one small step every day to move in that direction.

PART 4
WRAP UP

The daily grind doesn't have to kill your dreams—it just requires a different approach. Everything gets bigger when you eliminate the noise to discover what's possible in your life. All it takes is the inner conviction to consistently prioritize what matters to you. Don't wait for permission to want something more, better, or different in your life. The power to create the life you deserve is already inside you.

- **Nix the negatives** to create room for positivity and new possibilities.
- **Care more about less** to dedicate your time and energy to what matters to you.
- **Expand your worldview** to challenge your assumptions and broaden your thinking.
- **Find inspiration** to fuel your emotional energy, motivation, and actions.
- **Picture your future** to visualize your aspirations and make them more real.
- **Take aim** to discover more about where you want to go.

High-five yourself

Have you spent years downplaying your achievements, brushing off compliments, and moving straight to the next goal without pausing to acknowledge how far you've come? (Been there.) But here's what no one tells you: Celebrating your wins isn't selfish or arrogant—it's essential for your well-being. Every time you honor your progress, you reinforce the positive choices that got you there and create momentum for what's next. You're also giving yourself the recognition you freely give others, which helps you muster motivation during challenging times.

The world may have conditioned you to play small and be humble, but your wins deserve to be acknowledged and celebrated by the person who made them happen: you.

So make some noise!

Honor the big ones. When you land a new job, move to a new city, or hit a relationship milestone, mark the moment. A big win might call for a special night out or a wish-list purchase. Or you might just treat yourself to some quality time doing something you love. Whether you party out loud or inside your head, just make sure you party.

Acknowledge the small ones, too. It's easy to overlook small wins, but they're important because they add up to big wins over time.

Celebrating small wins builds momentum that propels you toward bigger goals. It also trains your brain to notice progress rather than what's still missing or incomplete. When you receive positive feedback from your manager, take a risk, make a friend, master a new skill, or stick to your exercise commitment, take note. Before your head hits the pillow, take one minute to jot down these wins in a journal or on your phone. Revisit your list of little wins at the end of the year or when you're having a bad day, and it will put a smile on your face—guaranteed.

Give yourself the credit you deserve for your achievements, big and small. Heck, give yourself extra credit!

Love Mondays

It can be hard to get yourself in gear on Monday mornings. Maybe you're still groggy after an action-packed weekend. Or you might be one of those people who spends part of Sunday dreading Monday. Or maybe you left a gnarly problem on your desk on Friday that's taking a while to wrap your head around again.

For various reasons, too many people think of Monday as something they have to endure so they can get to the good part of the week. Why squander 14 percent of your life? Monday is the secret weapon of high achievers and happy people everywhere. They love Mondays because they know it's a powerful opportunity to start fresh and make the most of the week ahead.

A Monday-loving attitude tees things up for you to:

Set the tone. Start with the small stuff—smile. This tiny gesture lifts your mood and the moods of the people around you. Make it a Monday morning ritual to have a quick check-in with a few coworkers to share your positive vibe. Do one fun thing every Monday (a fancy coffee splurge, a walk outdoors with a friend at lunchtime) so you always look forward to that little reward. The positivity and goodwill you bring to Mondays will give you a boost that lasts for days.

Own the week. No one wants to get whipped around by a week that's out of control before you even walk in the door on Monday! Get an early start and get organized for the week ahead. Write up a short agenda for your Monday before you leave the office on Friday so you don't have to start a new week cleaning up after the old one. This will also set you up to take actions you intend to take rather than just react to what will inevitably be flying at you come Monday.

Loving Mondays gives you an edge. Make the most of it!

Part 5

GET IN THE GAME

'FESS UP REST UP

UP SKILL UP POWER

POWER UP STAND UP

UP RAMP UP GEAR UP

PUMP UP 'FESS UP

UP OPEN UP RISE UP

STEP UP LIFT UP

MOVE UP FIRE UP

SHOW UP LEVEL UP

SPEAK UP MOVE

FESS UP REST UP

UP SKILL UP POWER

POWER UP STAND UP

Most successful professionals know something that others don't—and you won't find it in the employee handbook. They know that work is actually a game. It's a different kind of game, though, with unwritten rules, invisible scorekeepers, and prizes awarded to the "winners." Who are these mysterious winners? People who build strong relationships and make strategic moves to position themselves for advancement. They know how to play the game of work.

But before you can play the game, you need to get *in* the game. So why are so many people still sitting in the locker room? Some don't play the game because they don't realize a game is being played. They might be new to the work world and naively believe the workplace is a meritocracy. Others are aware of the game but refuse to play because they're annoyed that it's necessary. They want to be judged on their competence, not on how well they navigate the system. Some simply don't play because they're scared to join a game they don't understand. They recognize that forces are at work affecting their work experience, but they lack the skills—or guts—to face them.

People who don't play the game—for whatever reason—usually cross their fingers and hope their contributions will be noticed and rewarded. Unfortunately, this rarely happens because decision-makers are often unaware of their contributions, especially in larger organizations. Without visibility with leaders, many people miss out on promotions, raises, and other recognition they deserve. And these negative effects compound over time.

Don't let this happen to you. Become an active player in your career instead of a spectator on the sidelines. What does that mean? It means you stop waiting and hoping—you step up to the plate and take a swing. You cultivate relationships and use smart strategies that help you move up and advance your career. You believe in yourself so you bet on yourself. You know you can do hard things because you've done them before.

If you're one of those people who agonize over the "ick" factor of playing the game of work, here's some tough love: Get over it. You can maintain your integrity and bring your best, most authentic self to the game. Doing so is deeply satisfying and makes you feel powerful and in control of your future.

So how do you play a game with unwritten rules? The rules become clearer as you pay attention. Notice the invisible stuff that happens in every workplace—how promotions really work, the cultural code for acceptable behavior, who the decision-makers are, and who wields disproportionate influence with them. As your awareness grows, the game centers on being strategically and politically savvy to leverage relationships within your organization.

Once you're in the game, you discover possibilities you just can't see from the sidelines. You can build a reputation that protects you during organizational changes. You gain access to resources and opportunities that would otherwise be unavailable to you. Over time, you can even shape the work environment itself, potentially making it better for everyone.

Early in my career, I was reluctant to get in the game. It seemed like a distraction from the work I was doing. However, I failed to understand the invisible hierarchies and decision-making machinery that greatly affected my experience. As I watched my savvier coworkers rise, I realized that my own ignorance and indifference were causing me to miss out on opportunities, promotions, and money.

I was jolted into reality when I learned that a peer with the same experience, title, and role was being paid significantly more than I was. He had also just been handed another plum assignment with a marquee entertainment brand, while I was stuck working on the company's less glamorous outlet mall account. He was playing the game while I was watching (and resenting) him. That's when I decided I would stop being willfully blind to office dynamics. I needed to get in the game. When I finally did, I discovered five big things that shaped my career for many years to come:

Reputation is everything. How you're perceived by the people you work with is more important than the work itself. If they think well of you, doors open. If they don't, you're locked out. That's why your reputation is your most valuable professional asset.

In my 20s at the design firm, I worked in a small room with three guys who were about 10 years older than me. They were extremely talented and highly respected by other people in the firm due to their innovative work and the numerous industry awards they'd received over the years. While I could have allowed myself to be intimidated by them, instead I held my own. I discovered I could build my reputation with them by organizing our messy workspace, demonstrating my work ethic, meeting their high design standards, and speaking up in ideation sessions instead of quietly listening.

After a few months, I earned their respect, and eventually they became my friends, allies, and champions. Even better, their high regard for me positively influenced how others saw me and boosted my standing within the firm. Before long, my opinions were sought after and valued, and I was invited to join an influential task force for the firm.

Confidence is key. Promotions and great assignments don't always go to the people who are the most capable or deserving. They tend to go to the people who carry themselves with confidence.

I had to learn to project confidence by showing that I could take on difficult assignments, handle high-pressure situations with poise, and deliver high-stakes presentations to our CEO. Self-assurance convinces people you know what you're doing and makes them want to bet on you. And those moments when you don't feel 100 percent confident? Remember that other people often don't feel confident either (even if they act like they do).

Visibility is valuable. Working hard behind the scenes rarely leads to recognition for you. If you want your work to be recognized, it must be seen.

I was distraught when our firm won a major design award and my substantial contributions weren't acknowledged. I learned the hard way that I didn't just have to do great work; I also needed to actively promote it to the leaders and decision-makers in my company. So I got busy doing just that. I persuaded our internal communications team to feature my projects at the company's quarterly meetings, in the employee newsletter, and in the firm's promotional brochure. This exposure ensured that senior leaders knew about me and my work.

Internal networking gives you an edge. Most people think that meetings are where the action takes place at work. Yes, conference rooms and video meetings are playing fields. But the real internal networking happens in all the nooks and crannies of the rest of the workday—the hallways, the elevators, the Ubers, and the after-hours gatherings.

Networking doesn't necessarily require long conversations to build relationships. It often happens through spontaneous encounters in elevators or chats before or after meetings. I quickly realized that these informal interactions help establish rapport and trust with coworkers. I also found that I could connect with teammates and colleagues from other departments on Thursdays at the nearby pub, our go-to spot for happy hour.

Before long, we weren't just grabbing a beer once a week; we were chatting in the coffee room and taking walks during lunch. I started hearing about new clients in the pipeline, which allowed me to raise my hand for assignments before they were shared more broadly. I learned shortcuts for getting resources approved quickly and smart tips on tailoring a presentation to appeal to senior management. (They also supported me during my presentations.) My coworkers even taught me about the importance of the "meeting before the meeting"—previewing my work with stakeholders before a big meeting to avoid surprises. This is the kind of inside scoop that can give you a leg up.

Negotiation happens continuously. Negotiation doesn't end when you accept the job. You can ask for what you want and need at any point in your career.

For the first 15 years of my career, I didn't ask for much because I didn't know I could. I didn't ask for a signing bonus, extra vacation days, or leadership training. After experiencing burnout, I decided that my next job had to allow time for a personal life outside of work. My breakthrough moment occurred when I asked a potential new employer for a four-day workweek, and they agreed! Eventually, I learned that you can negotiate almost anything—flexibility, continuing education, attending conferences, travel, a home office stipend, and much more.

To play this game of work, you have to get into the thick of the action and mix it up with everyone on the field. You have to work up a sweat and sometimes get knocked around a bit. And occasionally, you have to make some big plays. I'm not talking about clocking in and out. I'm talking about something bigger—a career where strategic plays make a huge difference. Once I realized that work is a game and those who play tend to win more often, I jumped in with everything I had. Much like a Rubik's Cube, playing the game may be invigorating or maddening. To my great surprise, it was fun!

Are you ready to step *up* and get in the game?

27

Follow through

Be a rock.

If you order a latte at your favorite coffee shop and your drink is missing the oat milk or dash of vanilla you requested, you'd be annoyed with the barista. If this becomes a pattern of carelessness, you'll find a new place to go every day. In your own work, consistently dropping the ball or leaving loose ends may cost you customers, too. And worse, it could cost you career advancement and hurt your reputation.

It's not just completing the work you're assigned that counts—it's how you finish the job. Following through—carrying out each task, neatly wrapping up each project, and fulfilling every obligation without needing reminders or oversight—is the difference between work that's done and work that's done well. Doing what you say you're going to do is the essence of follow-through. In practice, this requires planning, attention to detail, and proactive communication.

Following through could give you an edge that builds trust and establishes you as a reliable colleague. When other people know they can count on you, you make their lives easier and less stressful. As a result, they will come looking for you to work on their projects, approve your requests more readily, and talk you up as a can-do, go-to resource.

A lack of follow-through impacts your credibility. Whether you've been juggling too many responsibilities to complete each one properly or you've just been unaware of the importance of following through, your standing is going to take a hit. Every unfulfilled commitment rapidly erodes trust. When someone else has to use workarounds to compensate for your shortcomings, they may not say anything to you about it directly, but your opportunities will quietly start to diminish.

If your follow-through is soft, here's how to make it rock solid:

Scope it. When making a commitment or receiving an assignment, confirm your understanding of what is required from beginning to end. Ask clarifying questions to ensure you understand expectations and get specifics about timing, including a final deadline and any milestone due dates along the way. Draft a short outline that captures these details and ask your manager for feedback. This feedback loop will help you get better at project planning and anticipating issues.

Plan your time. List the tasks and estimate how much time they will take you (double your estimate until you have enough experience with the task to plan accurately). Then block time for the tasks on your calendar to do the work. Managing your time and tasks is easier when you use the right tools. Your organization may be using project management applications such as Trello or Asana, or you might consider productivity tools such as Notion or Todoist, among countless others. Test a range of tools to determine what suits your work style.

Think ahead. Don't just think about the task that's currently in front of you. Anticipate what comes next, what could go wrong, or what else may be needed to complete the next task. Instead of constantly putting out fires, you're preventing them. This reduces your stress because you're always ahead, never behind.

Never assume. Pressing "send" is not a guarantee that your email or an important document was received. DM or make a quick call to confirm receipt. Check in with teammates who owe you a deliverable to ensure they're on track so your project stays on track. Confirm your client lunch is still on for tomorrow. Double-check that the key people you need in your project meetings have been invited and will attend.

Communicate regularly. Routinely provide project status updates to keep stakeholders in the loop (without them having to ask). Raise a yellow flag with your manager or project sponsor if your project hits a difficult patch or delay. Escalate quickly to your manager if a critical issue surfaces that you're not able or authorized to resolve. If requests from other people may impact your projects, ask your manager to help you prioritize your work to protect your project timelines.

Tie up loose ends. Wrap up all the details, whether it's drafting a final report, filing important documents, submitting an expense report, or transferring the next phase of work to someone else. Before you take time off, make a plan to prevent details from falling through the cracks in your absence. The final step of follow-through is recognizing other people's support and contributions. When you leave things on a positive note, it lets people know the work is complete and you value their efforts, and it reinforces that you're someone they want to work with again.

IRL

Samantha was relatively new in her role at the communications firm. She knew her new boss took a chance to hire her, as she didn't have the résumé of a typical marketing director candidate. Before taking the job, she had been a solo entrepreneur running her own apparel boutique, a demanding role that required her to handle marketing, operations, and finance and to follow through on every detail just to survive.

To build her reputation in her new role, Samantha employed a "surprise and delight" follow-through strategy she had used previously to win over customers in her store. Her first assignment was to develop a high-profile client event, and she made sure every detail was considered and well executed. To ensure event materials were top quality, she asked a team member to review final proofs in person with the printer instead of assuming they'd be fine. She tested the venue's sound system and lighting and arranged backup tech support. She made sure the clients had all of the logistical information they needed about transportation to the event, the awards dinner, and late-night happenings. She left a welcome bag in each event guest's hotel room that contained an event-branded water bottle, local snacks, a T-shirt, and a handwritten welcome note.

The event was a raging success. Samantha's fanatical focus on details thrilled the client and earned her props from her new boss.

Follow-through transforms good work into great work. By mastering the art of completion and attention to detail, you build a reputation as someone others can count on without question. This foundation of trust creates a positive cycle: The more reliable you are, the more opportunities will come your way, and the more fulfilling your work life will be. When you consistently follow through, your colleagues will notice, your career will flourish, and you'll discover the quiet confidence that comes from knowing you're someone people can always depend on.

Think about it 

Think about a recent project you were responsible for. Using a scale of 1 to 5, how would you rate your follow-through on that project (1 = terrible, 5 = excellent)?

Make a move

Name one area of that project where your follow-through could have been stronger. Commit to improving that aspect of your follow-through on your current or next assignment.

28

Ask for feedback

It's a learning accelerator.

Some people consider feedback the "f-word." To them, feedback is an uncomfortable discussion about their mistakes or shortcomings, so they avoid those conversations whenever possible. This often happens because they mistakenly believe that "feedback" only refers to negative comments about them or their work. Not true. Feedback includes both positive and negative input. Not surprisingly, most people find positive feedback energizing and motivating.

Maybe feedback is the "f-word" to you, too. Perhaps you've had a bad experience with feedback that makes you run the other way when you see it coming. But every time you avoid feedback, you deprive yourself of valuable information that could help you improve yourself. That's not a good play.

Feedback is an asset, not a liability. You need more feedback, not less. You want to seek feedback, not hide from it. Why? For starters, the world is changing fast, so you need to learn faster. Feedback is a quick way to gain valuable insights to help you continuously up your game. Think of it as a way to accelerate your learning.

There's more. Research shows that people who regularly seek feedback experience more creativity, greater job satisfaction, faster adaptation to new roles, and better guidance for future strategic decisions. And on a purely practical level, regular feedback lets you know how things are going and avoid surprises during your performance review.

Asking for feedback is key. Don't passively wait for it to come to you. First, it might not come when you need it. Second, asking puts you in control of getting the feedback that's most helpful to you. Third, if you don't ask, you might inadvertently convey that you're not committed to improving or learning. When you actively seek feedback, you show that you're serious about your work and invested in your performance.

Don't hide from feedback. Go out and get it! Here's how:

Get specific. Seek feedback that would be most useful to you. For example, you might want to improve your presentations, the quality of your work, or your communication skills. Ask for feedback in those specific areas and say, "*What can I improve next time?*" Avoid generic questions like "*How am I doing?*" or "*Do you have any feedback for me?*" They're too vague and put the burden on the other person to figure out what feedback will be helpful to you. Since nobody can read your mind, this will likely lead to a disappointing conversation.

Seek different perspectives. Your best friend at work might tell you one thing, while someone you don't know well in another department may tell you something different. Seek input from your manager, people at different levels and functions, even those with whom you have a prickly relationship, because they could have something valuable to share. Or check in with someone new to the team or organization, as they will have fresh eyes and may offer useful insights that others can't.

Pick your word. You don't have to use "feedback" if it isn't the right word for you or other people in your organization. Choose another word or phrase. Request "input" or "advice" or ask someone to be a "sounding board." You might refer to the conversation as a "development discussion."

Make it routine. Include feedback in your regular one-on-ones with your manager. Make it part of your agenda so you become more comfortable asking for and receiving feedback. Add "development discussion" as a standing agenda item and turn this conversation into a constructive tool for engaging with each other. After a big presentation, take a few moments to debrief with your team to find out what went well and what might be improved.

Time it well. If your feedback request is time sensitive, make that clear. Avoid catching someone in the hallway or pulling them aside after a meeting, as it puts the other person on the spot. Instead, ask, *"May I have 10 minutes of your time this week to get feedback on my presentation earlier today?"* Or better yet, let people know before the meeting that you're seeking their feedback and specify the topics that would be useful for you to hear about. This ensures they'll tune in and makes it easier for you to follow up after the meeting.

Receive it well. When you ask for feedback, some of it will inevitably be negative (HR calls this "developmental feedback"). If you're caught off guard, hurt, or overwhelmed, don't interrupt or get defensive. Stay calm and listen carefully to understand their perspective. If something is unclear, ask for clarification or examples. You could say, *"That feedback surprises me. Can you give me specific examples so I can better understand?"* Take notes so you can think about the details later and decide what to do with the feedback.

Express gratitude. It's important to end a feedback conversation by saying thank you, even if you've received challenging feedback and it feels hard to say those words. Saying thank you doesn't mean you agree with the feedback; it simply shows appreciation for the time, effort, and risk in providing it. After all, feedback may be just as uncomfortable to give as it is to receive. And giving feedback often indicates someone cares about you and wants to help you succeed. If saying thank you in the moment isn't possible, send a follow-up email to express your appreciation for their time and input.

Make a plan. When you receive feedback, you always have three options: 1) Accept all of it. 2) Disregard all of it. Or 3) Accept some and disregard some. Whatever you choose to do, be ready for the consequences. For instance, if you ask for feedback and consistently choose to disregard it, people will eventually become reluctant to provide it. Or you might ignore feedback you receive if you think it's unfounded, but this could give the impression that you have a negative attitude.

Consider these factors to guide your next step:

- Is the feedback consistent with what you've been told in the past? If you're unsure, seek additional perspectives from trusted colleagues to see if there's a pattern you were unaware of that you want to act on.
- Is the feedback core to your job, growth, or future advancement? If not, you might decide to give it lower priority.
- When you ask for feedback or advice, the person giving it likely expects you to take some action based on what they shared. Once you decide how to use the feedback, let them know your plan.

IRL

Nina was disappointed that her manager wasn't giving her helpful or actionable feedback. He'd say, "You're doing great. Keep doing what you're doing." She realized that his feedback was generic and not helping her grow, so she changed her approach. She added "growth opportunities" to their weekly touch-base agenda. Then she explained that her goal was to improve her communication effectiveness in team settings. She listed three specific areas she was focused on: active listening, nonverbal communication, and informal interactions. These topics were important to her because she was often nervous before meetings where she was expected to speak. She also felt uneasy with the chitchat before and after meetings and wasn't fully conscious of her body language.

Nina's specific and structured request showed her manager that she was eager to receive constructive feedback to support her in these growth areas. It took a while, but soon he was dialed in to what she was looking for. He advised her to arrive early to meetings to say hello to colleagues and ask about what they're working on. He explained that building rapport with them beforehand makes it less stressful to communicate with them later. He also advised her to relax and listen without worrying about what she might say next.

Nina seized these nuggets of feedback to improve her interpersonal communication. As an added bonus, she also strengthened her relationships with her team and manager.

When feedback becomes an integral part of how you work, it can become a powerful tool to support and guide you throughout your career. Your self-awareness increases, and your development path crystallizes in exciting ways you might not have ever foreseen. Even more, seeking feedback fosters trust and strengthens relationships with your colleagues.

Think about it 

What specific aspect of your work would benefit from feedback? Why is that feedback important to you?

Make a move 

Add a new feedback activity to your weekly routine with your manager or team.

29

Cultivate champions

Build your own board.

Nobody creates a successful career or life on their own. Literally nobody. Even superstar actors, athletes, company founders, and CEOs don't do it alone. They have teams of experts behind the scenes, paving the way for their greatness. While you might not have your own entourage (yet), there are lots of people in your life who would gladly offer support and root for you. You just have to identify the right people and ask them.

The right people are champions of you, your potential, and your future success. They might be men or women, inside or outside your organization, who serve as your behind-the-scenes "advisory team" and support system. Champions actively and eagerly listen to your professional aspirations and challenges. They provide a sounding board when you need it, they give you good ideas when you feel stuck, and they encourage you to take risks and go for it.

You may already have one or two of these champions in your orbit—maybe a great boss from your first job or a former colleague you've stayed in touch with. You could also consider a favorite professor, former client, or partner who knows your capabilities and has experienced your work firsthand.

One way to maximize the power of champions in your career is to develop your own "board." This small, diverse group of people can broaden your perspective, boost your confidence, and guide you as you navigate the highs and lows of work. This group will likely never meet or even need to know that they're on your personal board. It's an informal group—like a shadow cabinet—with whom you interact individually. In turn, you might offer to help them, which they will appreciate and you will enjoy. This strengthens the relationship, making it mutually beneficial.

This game-changing career move is called BYOB, short for "build your own board," and works best with some mix of this six-pack of champions:

Work friend. This is someone you can trust who will give you honest feedback and inspire you with a different way of looking at things. Gallup has long reported that having a best friend at work makes most people feel more satisfied, experience less stress, and have more fun. Yet only 2 out of 10 people claim to have a best friend at work. If "best friend" is an unreasonably high bar, having a work friend who can give you a reality check and serve as a sounding board is still valuable.

Mentor. This person is a well-respected, accomplished person (inside or outside your field or organization) who can offer guidance based on their experience, lessons learned, and knowledge of career paths and compensation packages. They will help motivate you, connect you to other professionals in your field, and avoid common mistakes. Meet with your mentor a few times a year to share career updates, progress on the items you last discussed, and new possibilities you're considering.

To test the waters with a prospective mentor, you might say, "*I admire your career and would love to learn from you. Would you be willing to spend 30 minutes with me a few times this year as part of my professional development?*"

Sponsor. This is a respected leader within your organization who has significant influence to go to bat for you when you're not in the room. These advocacy conversations happen with your manager, HR leaders, and executives when it's time to discuss new assignments, promotions, and pay increases. A sponsor is typically a senior leader with an eye out for high performers who are reliable and motivated to succeed.

Yet, according to *The Broken Rung*—authored by three female McKinsey senior partners who have each served as the firm's chief diversity and inclusion officers—women are overmentored and undersponsored in the workplace, impacting their career advancement. In fact, the authors reveal a sponsor can boost a woman's chance of getting promoted by roughly 10 percent. And because sponsors vouch for you, they use their credibility to build yours, so they are selective with who they back.

So how do you attract one? Start by seeking high-profile assignments that expose them to your work. If you don't yet have a relationship with a sponsor, reach out to introduce yourself and ask them for coffee to discuss your career aspirations. In that conversation, you could say, "*I admire your leadership and want to learn from you. Do you have an upcoming project I could be assigned to?*" or "*Would you consider advocating for me for the company's leadership development program?*" And if you're confident in your contributions and feel bold, you could say, "*Would you be open to sponsoring me? I really value your perspective and think your advocacy would be invaluable as I take on more responsibility.*"

Coach. A career coach is a professional guide who helps you navigate your career path. Working with a coach enables you to better understand yourself, see a broader range of current and future possibilities, handle difficult situations, set goals, and craft action plans.

Some organizations provide access to coaching or may pay for a coach as part of your professional development. One of the best ways to find a coach is through personal referrals. You might also tap into your university alumni network, professional associations, LinkedIn, or the International Coaching Federation to access a searchable database of coaches. There are numerous low-cost online coaching platforms such as BetterUp, Landit, and The Muse. A coach usually charges an hourly fee or offers a bundle of sessions over a period of three or six months. Choose a certified coach who has real-world business experience so their coaching accounts for the practical realities of navigating the workplace.

Industry peer. This is someone inside or outside your organization who has a job that is the same or similar to yours, who shares insights about their role and their experience in your field. You might meet an industry peer at an event or conference, or connect with them on LinkedIn. By cultivating this type of relationship, you may get tips on job opportunities outside of your organization and learn about compensation benchmarks.

To initiate a connection, you might say, "*Since we're in similar roles, would you be willing to connect periodically to exchange ideas on issues in our careers and current roles?*"

Cheerleader. This is your roommate, best friend, sibling, partner, or significant other—someone close to you who always has your back. They may help you think through a sticky situation or ask good questions. They may not be your go-to for specific job advice if they lack relevant experience, but their unconditional emotional support and willingness to listen may be just what you need sometimes. It's essential to be around people who are rooting for you to raise your energy level.

Use your board however best suits your needs, but always respect their time (and always arrive early, never late to meetings). Meeting in person, by phone, or via video call once every few months is a good cadence. You might also reach out to them when you're in a crisis and need a clear-headed perspective. Ask for advice on navigating a promotion or input when you're contemplating a major decision, such as taking a new job or going back to school. Remember to follow up with a thank-you after they've spent time with you and provided guidance or introductions to others in their networks. Tell them what you appreciated about the discussion and what actions you plan to take based on their insight.

Keep them engaged and interested in supporting your journey by sharing your wins. Send them a brief email or text to let them know your big presentation was a resounding success. Call them when you land that hard-earned promotion. They'll be delighted to celebrate your success and hear the excitement in your voice.

As your career unfolds, your board is likely to change or expand. An early mentor may be replaced by someone you connect with later in your career. You may cultivate a number of sponsors or industry peers over time. Genuinely nurture these relationships with small gestures by showing interest in their projects, sending birthday wishes, or congratulating them on their accomplishments. This will keep these relationships alive, vibrant, and in your corner.

IRL

Jacqueline had always navigated work on her own. As a busy single mom, she was used to being self-sufficient and resisted asking for help. She didn't want to burden anyone, and as a result, she isolated herself from relationships that could provide professional support or boost her reputation. Her peers began passing her by with bigger raises, promotions, and new job offers. This was maddening to Jacqueline, as she had the same skills and experience they did. She was determined to figure out what she needed to do to build her own career momentum.

Fortunately, Jacqueline had a former colleague who helped her think about her situation differently. She convinced Jacqueline that she would continue to struggle to advance if she didn't actively seek support in her workplace. Together, they worked out a plan for Jacqueline to connect with certain colleagues whose insight and assistance would be helpful now and as she explored her longer-term options.

She began by letting her manager know that she wanted to be on the path to promotion, which was information she'd never shared before. Next, she reached out to a peer who had recently been promoted to ask about how they'd made their case for advancement to management. Last, she emailed a senior leader who had been responsible for several projects Jacqueline had worked on over the last two years. She expressed her desire to move up in the company and asked to have coffee to seek their guidance. Impressed by Jacqueline's ambition and the quality of her work, the leader agreed to meet with her. After getting to know Jacqueline over the course of a year, the leader was glad to advocate for her with her manager, HR, and other leaders. Their behind-the-scenes influence helped her land a well-deserved promotion and a raise. And now Jacqueline had trusted resources in her corner for ongoing career-related guidance.

Your career is too important to navigate alone. Besides, it is much harder and less fulfilling when you're flying solo. When you have champions on your team, you're setting yourself up for success. You'll feel emboldened to put yourself out there and to take bigger chances. With a brain trust behind you, your confidence and your career can soar.

Think about it 

Name one person who championed you in the past. What impact did their support have on you?

Make a move 

List six people who would be ideal members of your personal board. Describe the specific support each of them could provide to you. Draft an email briefly explaining your request. Here's a sample email to adapt for yourself:

> *Dear [Name],*
>
> *You've been someone I've admired and learned from for many years. As I consider my career trajectory and important choices ahead, I would value your insight. Would you be open to spending 30 minutes with me every few*

months over the next year? I will come prepared with an agenda, commit to the action items we discuss, and keep you updated on my progress.

I'd welcome the opportunity to discuss this in more detail over coffee. I'm happy to meet at whatever time and location is convenient for you.

With gratitude,

[Your Name]
[Contact Info]

30

Pitch in (sometimes)

Help out when it helps you, too.

At work, you're expected to be a team player, especially when deadlines are looming and things need to be done. Yet many basic tasks that require time and cooperation don't necessarily fall under one person's job description, which is why it seems like someone's always looking for a volunteer to order office supplies, take meeting notes, onboard interns, or assemble event materials. These are essential activities in any office, but if they're routinely showing up on your to-do list, beware.

You have a finite amount of time and energy to complete your work. Whenever you agree to take on these kinds of tasks—a.k.a. the "office housework"—you have less time to do your real work. Yet saying no often doesn't feel like an option because you may seem uncooperative and risk disappointing your colleagues or manager. That hardly seems worth it, so you continue obliging.

Your repeatedly doing these necessary but thankless tasks benefits the organization, but not you. They get this essential work done without having to pay dedicated staff to do it, while you forfeit time you could be spending on your core responsibilities. This puts you at a disadvantage in a number of ways.

Not only is office housework time consuming, it falls squarely in the category of "non-promotable work," meaning work that doesn't contribute to your prospects for advancement. Oh, and chances are you're doing considerably more of it than your male colleagues. Research shows that women spend approximately 200 more hours annually on nonpromotable work than men in comparable positions. This adds up to more than a month you're *not* spending on your core responsibilities or new assignments. When it comes time for your annual performance review or promotion consideration, this invisible labor is rarely recognized or rewarded.

Every hour you spend organizing an office party is an hour you're not spending on visible, promotable work that advances your career and your reputation. So don't raise your hand every time there's office housework to be done. When you're known as the go-to person for these tasks, you'll be asked to do them again, which creates a pattern that's difficult to break. Here's how to be a high-value team player without getting trapped in a perpetual people-pleasing mode:

Spot the housework. Notice the nonpromotable tasks happening in your office. Identify any of these tasks that are keeping you from your core responsibilities. This could be mentoring interns, doing the morning coffee run for the team, or crafting the agenda for an internal task force. However, you may decide that some tasks, such as being a notetaker in an important meeting, are worthwhile because it keeps you in the loop with management on a project's next steps. By being aware of the tasks that don't have a strategic benefit to you, you can be prepared to decline by offering other solutions.

Suggest rotating or dividing the task. If you continue getting tapped to do office housework, suggest that you and other staff members take turns handling these tasks.

Alternatively, offer to handle a portion of the task. For example, you might agree to planning the office party if someone else handles the execution.

Propose alternative solutions. Suggest outsourcing administrative tasks such as collating and binding documents to a temporary worker or hiring an intern. Recommend the use of an AI tool for note-taking. If your boss asks you to do errands and pick up their kid from childcare while they're in a meeting, beware. You might be tempted to oblige one time, especially if they're in a pinch. This is risky because when you take on even one of these personal tasks, it usually leads to more of the same. Instead you could say, *"I'm not comfortable doing personal errands and childcare duties, but I'm happy to help you find a solution if this is urgent."* Then follow up later with a suggestion for a part-time personal assistant to handle ongoing personal tasks.

Keep track and communicate. No one else will keep track of the hours you spend on nonpromotable tasks, but you can. Then you will have something concrete to share with your manager to acknowledge the toll it's taking. You could say, *"You might not be aware that I am spending X hours each week doing office housework, which impacts my ability to deliver on my core projects and remain on the path to promotion. How can we work together to find a better solution for you, the organization, and me?"*

IRL

Even though Michelle was a senior manager, her boss frequently asked her to pick up coffee, organize the supply closet, and order lunch for the team. He'd even ask her to make copies in the middle of a meeting. Every time this happened, she felt torn. If she said no, she might disappoint or even anger her manager. When she said yes, she missed out on important discussions while she was out of the room. She was worried about how these tasks were impacting her own potential for growth and advancement.

She finally worked up the courage to have a conversation with her manager. "You might not be aware that I've been spending nearly eight hours a week on office housework. This breaks my concentration and prevents me from working on critical projects at top capacity. You know I'm always glad to help the team, but these tasks are taking time away from my primary job responsibilities as well as my growth and development. Can we find a way to shift them to someone else?" Her manager hadn't realized Michelle was shouldering so many of these tasks. She was a valuable member of the team, so her boss agreed to test a new approach.

The manager tapped a new employee to take on the work. She was a recent college graduate who was eager to assume more responsibility and get exposure to more senior colleagues. It took some adjustments for everyone, but the new solution was a win-win-win. The work got done, the new hire saw more action, and Michelle was able to give her full attention to her top priorities.

You can be seen as a well-respected team player without taking on menial tasks outside your main responsibilities. When you're strategic about lending a hand or can persuade others that a different approach is better, you up your game. This benefits both the organization and you. The task will either be reassigned or deprioritized. You're freed up to excel at your work, rack up your accomplishments, and shine in your next performance review.

Think about it

How much time do you spend each week on office housework that isn't part of your primary responsibilities?

Make a move

Speak to your manager about the tasks that distract you from your priorities. Suggest an alternative that would remove the most time-consuming of these tasks from your workload. If your manager resists, ask if your solution could be tested for a 90-day period.

31

See the whole field

Connect the dots in every direction.

Picture yourself sitting in front of a chessboard. If you play the game thinking about just the chess piece that's in your hand and the one move you're about to make, you'll likely lose. But if you look at the entire board, considering how each piece relates to the other and anticipating multiple moves ahead, you can craft a winning strategy.

The workplace is a lot like that.

Just showing up for work every day, keeping your head down, and doing your best on the work assigned to you is not enough to ensure your advancement. To get ahead, you have to be able to see beyond your own role and responsibilities and understand how what you do fits into the larger picture. When you see the whole field of play, you know how decisions are made, who has influence, and how the organization makes money. You are aware of your organization's position in its industry, and you get what senior leaders are doing to pursue the organization's objectives. This information enables you to plug into the action happening in every direction, at every level of the organization. As your instincts sharpen, you can see the pieces on the board, the moves you can make, and where you can jump in the game.

Seeing the whole field means having a solid grasp of your organization's structure, business model, and strategic priorities, as well as its mission, vision, and values. It also means having a clear picture of how your work supports and relates to these factors. Do you know how your work helps the organization meet its business objectives, grow sales or profit, and elevate its brand? Do you embody the organization's values and contribute to a strong culture? When you're conscious of these dynamics, you'll ask better questions, facilitate insightful conversations with your colleagues, and have more overall impact.

Here's how to zoom out and see the whole field:

Absorb the messaging. Notice what senior leaders say internally (quarterly updates, monthly financials, or town halls) and externally (press releases, website updates, and annual reports). These messages signal what's important and where to focus your efforts.

Learn the business. Understand how the organization generates revenue, attracts and retains customers, and distributes its products or services. Connect organizational messaging to the work you're doing. Consider how your projects help deliver against the organization's priorities, such as growing revenue, cutting costs, or serving new customer segments. If you are unsure how your work fits into the bigger picture, ask your manager to clarify. This understanding makes articulating your value during a performance review a more straightforward exercise.

Manage your manager. Sometimes called "managing up," this means actively building a productive working relationship with your boss that benefits both of you. Rather than hoping they'll intuitively understand what you need, take ownership of making the relationship work.

Understand their priorities and how your work contributes to their success. Ask about their primary objectives for the quarter and identify where your goals can directly support theirs. Learn their style by asking how they want you to communicate. You could ask, *"Would you prefer I summarize project status in daily Slack messages, weekly email recap, or biweekly in-person meetings? Do you prefer text or a phone call for emergencies?"*

Once you get their rhythm, you can start anticipating what they'll need from you and give them a heads-up before problems become disasters. Be proactive about communication and make their life easier when you can. When you do this well, you'll find that your boss becomes an advocate for you rather than just someone who assigns tasks and checks in occasionally.

Connect at your level. Show genuine interest in getting to know your teammates and colleagues from other departments. Ask about their weekend plans or grab coffee together. Get to know their projects and find out where they might need help. Be collaborative, not competitive. Share knowledge and resources freely and find ways to add value to their work. Your ongoing generosity will pay off when you need their support in the future.

Connect above your level. Find ways to get close to decision-makers. Ask thoughtful questions about the organization's priorities with skip-level leaders (e.g., your boss's bosses) in town hall or department meetings. Seek out project assignments that key leaders are involved with, attend their talks, or try to speak with them at events. Show you're paying attention to what matters to the organization and find brief moments (in the hallway, elevator, or the end of a meeting) to mention how your work and your team's work is making a difference. You could say, *"I'm excited about our company's focus on growth. My team has been working on a compelling campaign to attract new customers. I'd be happy to share the early feedback after it launches."*

When you build relationships with people more senior than you, they will appreciate your efforts to impact the business and are more likely to remember you or seek you out for high-visibility projects. These relationships may also prove valuable when promotions are being considered and you need an advocate behind closed doors.

Connect below your level. Recognize that it takes all types of roles to make the organization successful. Be kind and appreciative to everyone, including those who don't work on your team or in your department—and especially to junior staff, interns, or admins. Remember their names, give them credit, and listen to their ideas. This is a great way to get a read on the organization's morale and convey to them that their contribution is important. Help them understand how the business works. Do what you can to support them to do their job well and advocate for their growth and development. By connecting with people more junior than you are, you will develop mentoring and leadership skills while cultivating relationships that may be valuable to you both someday.

IRL

Camilla had a great relationship with her direct reports, who thought she was a great manager. But her peers and manager thought otherwise. Camilla was given low marks on her teamwork with management and business impact in her recent performance review, and she was baffled. "My team loves me!" she exclaimed. She wasn't seeing the whole field. She was on an island with a devoted team, focused only on her department's priorities. However, she forgot that part of her role is working collaboratively with senior leader peers, achieving company priorities, and helping her manager succeed.

This was eye-opening to Camilla, as she had been showing up each day thinking only about her own work and how to best support her team. She wasn't investing time or energy in building peer relationships in other departments and didn't realize its importance. She hadn't even considered how partnering with other leaders could drive more revenue and lead to solutions that improved profitability, too. This lack of effort meant her work wasn't considering the full spectrum of inputs it needed from creative, technology, and finance leaders.

Camilla also hadn't considered her manager's priorities and how she could contribute or remove some of the burdens, freeing up her manager's time for other priorities.

Once she became aware of these dynamics, Camilla changed her approach. She explained to her team that it would take away some of her time devoted to them, but seeing the bigger picture would help her and them have a more meaningful impact on the business, and their careers would benefit, too.

When you see the whole field and all the forces at work in an organization, you'll become a bigger, more valuable player. You will see a multitude of opportunities to make your mark that people who aren't playing will never see. You'll notice that senior leaders are eager to involve you in bigger and bigger stuff. So when you play at a higher level, you not only move the business forward, you catapult your career, too.

Think about it

How does your work contribute to the organization's business goals? Which relationships do you need to develop or strengthen at your level, above your level, and below your level?

Make a move

Each month, focus on one relationship to build or strengthen within the organization. This might be with a peer, senior leader, or junior team member. Consider using your organization's business goals or priorities to guide your conversations.

32

Promote yourself

Advocate for your own advancement.

If you just sit at your desk, quietly waiting for someone to tap you on the shoulder and say, "Congratulations, you've been promoted," you could be sitting there waiting for a very long time. Advancement rarely happens by chance. Most often, it happens when you've done these three things right:

- You've communicated to your manager that you want to be on the path to promotion.
- You've excelled in your job and acquired the skills, relationships, and experience you need to succeed at the next level.
- You know the criteria and have made a clear, convincing case for your promotion.

This just means being proactive. You don't assume your manager knows you want to advance. You prepare yourself to take on a bigger role. And you do your homework to sell it.

You're sure you're ready to take on a bigger role, but will your organization see it the same way? Many organizations start by considering where you are in relation to these three stages of growth:

- **Developing:** When you're new to the role and learning how to deliver (0–12 months).
- **Performing:** When you're consistently delivering and meeting expectations (6 months or more).
- **Mastering:** When you're routinely exceeding expectations and can teach someone else the role (1–3 years or more). Most organizations require mastery before you'll be considered for promotion. Some expect you to be doing some or most of the next-level job before you're promoted as evidence that you can handle the role.

Every organization's milestones or requirements for promotion are different, but you can use this general measure to assess your promotion readiness from their point of view and build a winning case for yourself.

When you advocate for your own advancement, you are more likely to be promoted. If you're shy about it, don't be surprised if it doesn't happen. Self-advocacy is not bragging or front-running. It's simply a practical necessity. Managers have many responsibilities, and you are just one of them. It's possible they're not aware of all your contributions, or they may not be thinking about whether you're on a path to promotion until you bring it to their attention. And no one knows your value better than you.

Here's how to start moving yourself along:

Understand the process and requirements. Every organization is different, so know how yours works. Some organizations promote once yearly, semiannually, or quarterly; some don't have a predetermined schedule. In some organizations, there has to be an open role for you to be promoted to.

Ask HR what specific requirements you need to meet, such as managing a certain number of people, hitting revenue targets, or demonstrating particular competencies. Also ask exactly when promotion recommendations must be submitted by managers and when decisions are made. For example, if promotions are announced in early February, they were most likely approved in December or January and submitted by managers in October or November. So have your conversation with your manager well in advance of their deadline.

Know your path. Read the job descriptions of potential roles you could work toward and understand the promotion criteria for each. Ask your manager or HR representative pointed questions like, "*What milestones or metrics would demonstrate that I'm ready for promotion?*" or "*What additional responsibilities could I take on to position myself for advancement?*" In a smaller or more flexible organization, you might offer to draft your own professional development plan. This plan would outline particular skills and experience you intend to acquire, and how and on what timeline you would do this. If the role you envision doesn't yet exist, you could also offer to draft a job description.

If your manager or HR representative doesn't know what a path to promotion looks like, find someone more senior in the business who is familiar with your work and ask for their guidance. If nobody in your organization can define your path to promotion, that's a sign that upward mobility might not exist there.

Track your wins throughout the year. Spend a few minutes each week logging your accomplishments and accolades you receive on a "hype sheet." Having current documentation of your contributions and impact makes it easy to prepare for a performance review and a promotion-readiness conversation.

Make your aspirations known. Schedule a meeting with your manager to discuss your career goals. If you're unsure of what's possible, but you want them to know you want to advance and need their help figuring out the path, you might say, "*I'm eager* *to contribute to the organization and advance into a role with more responsibility. What does the path to a promotion look like for me?"*

Or if you know exactly what you want and what's required to get there, you might say, *"I envision being a general manager in the next three to five years. Here's my understanding of what I need to do to get there. Does that sound right?"*

Also share your desire for upward mobility with your sponsor or mentor and ask for their guidance on advancement. They may have insider tips on how to acquire the skills you need or the best way to make your case. If they know what you're after, your sponsor may be in a position to advocate for you with decision-makers.

Prepare your case. To persuade your manager to support your promotion, you need to present them with convincing evidence. This includes a detailed, written account of your major contributions, new skills you've developed, certifications you've acquired, and endorsements you've received from colleagues. Organize this information in a way that makes sense to your manager, whether by project, job responsibilities, or strategic initiatives. Provide as much detail as possible about the quantifiable impact you've had on the organization, your department, and your team's success. Some organizations ask that you submit a written self-assessment in advance of the meeting with your manager, so be sure to know what is expected.

Be direct. Once you've made your case to your manager, ask directly, *"Do I have your support for a promotion?"* If yes, inquire about next steps and timing. If no, you could ask, "*What would I need to work on to be considered in the foreseeable future?*" Or you could say, "*That's disappointing. Help me understand what's influencing your decision.*" They may not be able to support your promotion due to a hiring freeze or other obstacles outside of their control. Or they may be resistant to your promotion because their job is easier if you remain in your current role. If they make it clear they can't (or won't) agree to advocate for your promotion now or in the future, you've probably hit a dead end with your manager. It may be time to look elsewhere—inside or outside your organization—to find a path to advancement.

Document the conversation. Send a follow-up email to your manager so you have a record of what was discussed. Let them know you plan to share it with HR so they are in the loop. Write a summary of the conversation and next steps. Begin by thanking them for their time and guidance, then briefly recap the key requirements and expectations discussed to ensure you're on the same page. Outline the specific actions you committed to taking, along with any agreed-upon timelines, and confirm what your manager (or HR) will do on their end. Include any clarifying questions that arose after the meeting, and express your enthusiasm for the development plan. Keep the tone appreciative but businesslike, and focus on concrete next steps rather than rehashing the entire conversation. It could go something like this:

> *Hi [Name].*
>
> *Thank you for taking the time to discuss my career progression today. I found our conversation very helpful in understanding the path forward.*
>
> *Based on our discussion, I understand that [summarize two or three key requirements/expectations]. I'm committed to [specific actions you'll take] over the next [time frame].*
>
> *I have one follow-up question about [specific item], and I wanted to confirm that we'll reconnect in [agreed time frame] to assess progress.*
>
> *I appreciate the guidance and look forward to working toward these goals.*
>
> *With gratitude,*
>
> *[Your Name]*
> *[Contact Info]*

This approach shows you're organized, committed to follow-through, and serious about your professional development while creating a written record of the agreed-upon path forward.

IRL

Ursula got a big salary bump when she transitioned to a sales support job after working as a public school teacher for many years. For eight years in this role, she received positive feedback at each annual performance review, but she was never promoted. She was making much more money in this role than she did as a teacher, so she felt grateful. She didn't feel comfortable asking for more, even though she saw her peers getting promoted. The more she wondered why she wasn't recognized for her efforts, the more agitated she became. She finally summoned the courage to ask her boss what it would take to get promoted, and she was surprised when he responded, "I wasn't aware that was important to you. Let's talk about it."

He assumed she liked her role and wasn't eager for more responsibility. He also assumed that she wouldn't want to relocate for any of the open, more senior positions she was qualified for because she had a toddler at home. He reached these erroneous conclusions because Ursula had never shared her aspirations with him.

Once they had an open conversation about her goals, they arrived at a development plan that would allow her to be considered for a promotion in the next cycle. This energized Ursula because she could see exactly the steps she needed to take and was committed to documenting her weekly progress.

If you're serious about advancing your career, don't leave it to chance. Your organization needs what you bring, but they can only fully benefit from it if you make it impossible for them to ignore you. Recognize that strategic self-advocacy increases your chances of getting what you want and deserve. So be bold and unapologetic. Make a smart plan and go all out. After all, good things don't come to those who wait—they come to those who act.

Think about it

Is your manager aware of your career aspirations? If not, why not?

Make a move

Research your path to promotion within your organization. Develop a plan by outlining a detailed strategy to meet promotion criteria. Discuss it with your manager and ask if you have their support for promotion.

33

Make the ask

Your silence hurts you.

When you don't ask for what you want, it costs you. Every time you don't make an ask—whether it's to work remotely, be assigned a challenging project, get a raise, or be promoted—it's pretty much guaranteed those things won't happen.

Here's a hard truth: Organizations don't often reward silent employees. They reward visible, high-impact contributors who advocate for themselves. They recognize, accommodate, and advance people who confidently communicate their value to the organization and clearly express their needs. "Making the ask" is a fundamental skill in the game of work. It's like parallel parking or downloading an app—your options are severely limited when you don't know how to do it. And yet many women struggle to ask for what they want. Why?

Asking for anything may be difficult, especially for a woman who fears being perceived as demanding or difficult. Unfortunately, she's got good reason to worry about that.

According to a 2016 McKinsey report, women negotiate for promotions and pay raises as often as men do but are 30 percent more likely than men to receive feedback that they are "intimidating," "too aggressive," or "bossy." It's no wonder so many women keep their asks to themselves at work. No one wants to be shunned or labeled as unlikable.

But not asking for what you want hurts you more than asking for it ever could. When you don't make an ask, you get nothing. When you do make an ask, there's at least a chance you'll get something from it. And when you make an ask well, you're more likely to get exactly what you're looking for. That's the home run, the touchdown, the game-winning goal. Here's how to finesse making an ask:

Know your audience. Make sure you know who to ask. Most conversations begin with your manager, although depending on the organization and the ask, some could begin with HR. No matter what you are seeking, you will have more leverage if you're in good standing with your manager. It makes getting a yes to more resources, a new title, flexible hours, or a promotion easier when you have their support.

Find the right time. You're more likely to get what you want if you make an ask at the right moment. This could be after the successful completion of a project, or after the company has reported positive quarterly earnings or strong annual results. If you've received an advanced degree, earned an important certification, been exceeding expectations in your role for six months or more, or been doing double duty (your job and an open role) for an extended period, it may be a good time to make an ask. You may also have more success when leaders are concerned about retaining high performers during a crucial time.

There is also a wrong time to make an ask. For example, if your boss is in a foul mood or the organization is in crisis or under pressure to meet its numbers to please investors.

Find the right tone. Be confident without apologizing for wanting more. So don't start with "*I'm sorry to bother you*" or "*I know this might be a lot to ask.*" You've earned the right to have this conversation, so frame it as a business case. Be assertive, not aggressive. Be firm but warm. Try, *"I'd like to discuss my role and career progression. I've consistently exceeded my targets and have taken on additional responsibilities for the last year. I have also been performing many of the duties of the role above me, which has helped the department meet its goals more quickly."* Focus on what you have accomplished and how it's added value, not just how hard you've worked.

Never make major asks (e.g., raises, promotions, special work hours, requests for resources) by email or instant message, because your tone may be misconstrued. Face-to-face conversations always have better outcomes.

Approach it like a win-win. Think about how your ask will benefit you and your organization. If you get more resources, you'll drive more sales. If you get a stretch assignment, you'll grow and become more valuable to the organization. If you work remotely, you'll have more time to work without interruption on your projects. If you are promoted into a new role that has more responsibilities and direct reports, you'll have the bandwidth to be more productive and impactful. Remember, you're not asking for a favor; you're making a case for why your ask makes good business sense.

Practice, practice, practice. Don't wing it, as this rarely goes well. Write out, record, or role-play your conversation in advance. This way you can consider possible objections and be self-assured in your delivery. Avoid subjective statements such as "I believe" or "I feel" and use specific, objective language instead. For example, *"I need a summer intern to manage administrative tasks to free up my time for the new product launch"* or *"I would like to attend the upcoming industry conference so I can stay current on trends that will help inform our annual planning session."*

Here's a pro tip: Memorize the first two sentences of your ask so you can make good eye contact at the outset. Make your ask and then stop talking. Endure the awkward silence that may happen and wait for a response. (Seriously. Zip it. Not a word.)

Close the conversation. Don't leave it open-ended. Ask, *"Are we on the same page to proceed?"* If they are unable or unwilling to make a decision in the moment, ask for a specific date for a decision (one or two weeks is usually reasonable) and schedule a short follow-up meeting on that date. This demonstrates follow-through and also your seriousness about the ask.

Follow up. Within 24 hours, send an email that summarizes the conversation, reiterates your ask, and spells out the next steps. If your ask was not approved in the meeting, mention that you will schedule the follow-up meeting to discuss your manager's final decision. If you get a new boss, share this documentation as part of their onboarding.

Have a backup plan. If you get a no, express your disappointment and understanding by saying, "*That's disappointing to hear. I understand you're in a difficult position.*" Then ask the pivotal question: "*What kind of flexibility do you have?*" They might have something in their back pocket to offer you, so hear them out.

If they don't offer you something, be prepared to ask for something else that's important to you. Yes, you want the number one thing on your list, but it doesn't always go that way. So know what else you might accept as your consolation prize. Consider things that might be easy for them to say yes to or would have a low cost to the organization. For example, the easier ask could be a new title, more PTO, a home office stipend, or an industry membership. Give this thought in advance of the conversation so you aren't grasping for ideas in the moment. Then ask to revisit the decision about your original ask in three months.

IRL

When Melanie discovered she was making less money than her peers in similar marketing operations roles, she was furious. She marched into her manager's office and said, "I've just learned I am underpaid. My rent has skyrocketed, and I feel I deserve a raise." The manager stared at her, annoyed by this (irrelevant) declaration, giving Melanie the distinct impression that a raise was out of the question. Humiliated, Melanie stormed out. She didn't get a raise, and her relationship with her manager became strained.

After cooling down, she realized she had mishandled the situation. She wanted to try again, so she called a mentor to help her think through a more constructive approach. Later, she scheduled a meeting with her boss and prepared a reasonable and measured statement of her ask:

"Thank you for making time for this important conversation. First, I apologize for mishandling our earlier meeting on this subject. I'm prepared to have a constructive discussion with you today.

I want to start by saying how much I enjoy my work and being part of this company. I've been able to develop process efficiencies that have lowered our department's operating costs by 11 percent. I've researched salaries in our industry and learned that I am currently being paid 15 percent below the benchmark for my role, level, and company size. I'm asking for an increase of 15 percent that addresses this deficiency and recognizes the value I'm bringing to the team and company."

While impressed by her argument, Melanie's manager wasn't in a position to approve the request immediately. But she was able to work with Melanie to document her contributions for HR to consider for a salary adjustment. This ultimately resulted in a raise that made Melanie's compensation comparable to her peers.

Getting what you want requires you to have the courage to step forward and make an ask on your own behalf. This is an important and healthy expression of self-respect. You don't have to wait for all the stars to align perfectly to make it happen. You just have to make a great ask, with conviction. While the answer might not always be yes, asking changes something fundamental—it establishes that you know what you want and are willing to ask for it, making the next conversation easier. And when you do get that yes, it's because you created the opportunity, not because you waited for someone to notice you deserved it. When you ask for what you need, want, or deserve, you don't just increase your chances of getting it—you increase your skill at getting it.

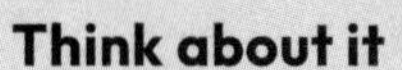

Think about it

What ask do you want to make?

Make a move

Develop the script for your ask and practice with a friend or mentor. Then schedule the meeting and go for it!

34

Become a force

Drive positive change.

Most people think that change in the workplace comes from the top down or the bottom up. In fact, sometimes the most profound and lasting change comes from forces somewhere in the middle of an organization.

These forces are the people who positively influence the culture by bringing energy and new ideas to the organization. They understand what makes the place tick and are tuned into the needs of the people they work with. They have empathy. They have great relationships at every level and are respected for what they do to improve the work environment for everyone. They set a positive tone in difficult situations. And their attitude and enthusiasm make other people want to be a part of whatever they're doing.

Simply put, a force makes good stuff happen.

That good stuff happens because a force knows how to translate their big ideas into actionable plans. They also know how to navigate office politics and get their teams and bosses excited to be on board. They boldly take initiative and are not afraid to fail. They don't daydream about doing something; they roll up their sleeves and do it.

Chances are you've known a force or two during the course of your work life. They really make a difference, don't they? Well, that force could be you! If you care deeply about your organization and the people you work with, you could be a force. If you see solutions where everyone else sees problems, you could be a force. If you believe your role can be bigger than just the bullets on your job description, you could be a force.

When you're a force, you can have a powerful impact on the business and the culture, which is a big-time benefit to the organization for which you'll likely be rewarded. But you'll discover you don't do it for the recognition; you do it for the indescribable satisfaction of being a catalyst for positive change. And there's no better feeling in the world than that.

Here's how to find the force in you:

Look around. Notice inefficiencies and common frustrations—these are the workplace realities that cause the most stress and discontent. What are the short-term workarounds teams have adopted without landing on a long-term solution? These are good indications of pain points where you might advocate for a new and better approach.

Be idea oriented. Develop inclusive solutions, such as a new process or policy, that would ease the pain for everyone. Consider how you could make people's day-to-day lives better. Think "if only . . . " If only there was a better way to organize this project. If only there was a policy that allowed new parents to ease back into work. If only more voices were heard in every meeting. If only there was a green solution to our office waste. Consider how technology might play a role that hasn't yet been considered.

Get a green light. Most organizations don't appreciate when you start working on something new that's not part of your core job responsibilities. Share your idea with your manager and highlight the benefit it will bring to the organization. That could be making something more efficient, saving money, or improving the culture. Ask for their support to spend X hours on it per week instead of low level, nonurgent tasks. You could ask, "*Is this idea worth pursuing?*" With your manager's buy-in, you could ask, "*Can you help me get access to a small budget or a couple of people to get started?*"

Start small. Make a prototype and test it. Introduce an improvement for one team or project and see how it goes. If the feedback is positive, you will have early champions and find it easier to develop your prototype into a bigger project within your department. If you continue to experience success, you might expand to other departments or divisions. Having an impact can take time and patience for the results to be experienced by the people you work with.

Recruit other change agents. Find other people inside the organization who are willing to help you. Tap into their influence or connections for a bigger test or to gather more feedback. Once people are talking about the good things happening, more people are likely to get involved.

Being a force doesn't require a gregarious, outgoing personality; anyone with a good idea and a positive attitude can make a difference. Wherever you sit within your organization, there are opportunities to use your insight, empathy, and relationships to drive change. And you don't need the authority that comes with a big job title to do it. You just need to believe in yourself and your big idea!

IRL

Marti happily participated in the company's mentoring program and benefited from the guidance she received. During these sessions, she noticed that many of the leaders in her company were stressed out by AI—how to keep up with it and use it, if at all. As a former social media content creator, she was extremely interested in AI and had taken courses and subscribed to countless podcasts and newsletters on the topic.

Marti decided to organize a small group of "techies" from within the organization to develop a brief for senior leaders that summarized emerging technologies, current applications, and future possibilities. She shared the brief with her manager, who thought it was tremendously helpful. She then suggested an optional monthly lunch-and-learn for senior leaders in the organization. Many who attended quickly felt more confident making decisions about utilizing this technology. Marti's little project quickly expanded from a brief to a monthly presentation that ultimately paved the way for a reverse mentoring program in her company. What a force!

When you step up as a force in your workplace, you're doing more than a job—you're changing the DNA of the organization you work for. You're making work better for everyone. It's massively gratifying knowing you've made something important better. It makes you fall in love with what you do. And that love—for the work, for the impact, for the people around you—that's what transforms an ordinary career into an extraordinary one.

Think about it 

Recall a difficult situation at work that was causing distress or frustration for your team or department. What, if anything, did you do to help? What, if anything, would you do differently now?

Make a move 

Think of a current problem you might have a creative solution for. Test your idea with a small group of people who would benefit from this improvement. If it works, share the results with your manager to discuss how it could be applied elsewhere in the organization.

PART 5
WRAP UP

When you get in the game, you understand how your work fits into the bigger picture. You make smarter decisions about where to focus your energy, how to grow your skills, and which opportunities to pursue. You build strong relationships up, down, and across the organization that support what you want to accomplish. You discover that the most successful professionals aren't necessarily the most competent or patient. They don't wait for opportunities to find them or apologize for expressing their desires. They go after what they want with gusto.

- **Follow through** to build credibility as someone reliable and trusted.
- **Ask for feedback** to accelerate your growth.
- **Cultivate champions** to support, guide, and celebrate your success.
- **Pitch in (sometimes)** to help the organization when it helps you, too.
- **See the whole field** to connect the dots and navigate up, down, and across the organization.
- **Promote yourself** to showcase your impact and express your aspirations.
- **Make the ask** to increase the chances of getting what you want, need, and deserve.
- **Become a force** to drive positive change for yourself and others.

Pass it on

Too many people delay giving back until the end of their careers or lives. Don't be one of them. There is no perfect moment, age, or income level at which to share your time, expertise, or money. The uncertainties of life mean that the opportunities to give that you have today may not be possible for you tomorrow, making today's small kindness infinitely more valuable than tomorrow's big intentions.

Also your generosity will mean more to you and other people if it happens consistently throughout your life. For you, it reinforces your values and reflects who you are as a person. For others, regular generosity creates lasting impact by showing them they matter enough to receive continued care and attention rather than just an occasional gesture. And as an added bonus, it may inspire someone else to be generous, too.

If you're asking yourself, *What can I give?* you may be surprised to discover just how much you have to offer at whatever stage of life you're in.

Give what you are able to give. If you have more money than time, donate to organizations that align with your values. Even if money is tight, try budgeting just $5–10 deducted from your paycheck. This will benefit causes or groups you care about supporting now and provide a gateway for deeper engagement down the road. You'll feel psychologically invested in their success, knowing the collective impact of small, regular donations.

Offer your time. If you have more time than money, consider volunteering in your community. Participate in the job fair at the local high school or spend time reading to seniors or doing their errands. Help care for animals at the nearby shelter or consider fostering a pet. Show up as an extra pair of hands at a food bank, soup kitchen, or tree planting. Bring genuine eagerness to any task you're assigned.

Share what you know. If you have particular expertise, find a way to share it. You could give a presentation to one of your organization's employee resource groups, post an instructional video on social media, build a course, or give a talk to the staff at your favorite local nonprofit organization. You might mentor students at your local school who need support or would be inspired by hearing about your career journey. Or you might reverse mentor someone more seasoned than you who would appreciate your unique perspective, cultural insights, or social media skills.

When you give back now and throughout your life, you not only provide timely help to those who need it, but science shows it will make *you* happier! (Psst . . . pass it on!)

One more thing

If you've arrived at this page, I hope it's because you've devoured all the chapters of this book. Maybe you've made some surprising discoveries about yourself. You might have found new ways you want to grow or new skills you'd like to develop. Perhaps you've navigated some tricky conversations using the scripts and tips. Or maybe you recognized some of your own challenges in the IRL stories. If you've already taken some bold steps and experienced profound transformation from what you've learned here, you've made my wildest dreams come true!

If you're hesitant or don't feel ready to try these strategies yet, that's okay. But know there's no such thing as being 100 percent ready. Your growth will only happen when you move—especially when you're scared (trust me on this).

You build momentum through action, not idling. Just move. Even a small step on days you don't feel like moving still creates progress that fuels your confidence. Those small steps lead to bigger steps. And big steps lead to breakthroughs and life-changing moments that elevate your career and life. No matter the size of the step, all of them will count. You're in control of your career and living the life you've chosen for yourself.

As your life unfolds, show the world you have something to offer that nobody else can—your unique blend of lived experience, strengths, and insights. This special combo will also include what matters to you, what you care about, and how you connect with others. When you bring all these elements together to shape your career and life choices, you'll discover what it feels like to level up. You'll unlock your potential and feel energized and fulfilled. (And that feels pretty freakin' great.)

The world needs more women in positions of leadership, influence, and power. The world needs *you*. What you do for yourself not only benefits you but also helps the woman sitting next to you and countless other women in your organization or community who are looking for hope, opportunities, and ways to move up in work and life. You are their guiding light. So keep shining!

As you rise, you'll see old systems that need to be dismantled so that new ones—better ones—can be built. The workplace needs new systems so that organizations can evolve, new leaders can emerge, and everyone can get a fair shot. This will enable more individuals to expand their desire and capacity to contribute and increase their earning potential. (Won't that be incredible?)

If you have moments of doubt or encounter pushback, remember this: You deserve the career and life you want. You deserve to flourish and reap the rewards of your hard work. Repeat it to yourself: *I deserve this.* However, hard work alone won't make it happen. It will happen when you lead yourself and stop waiting for others to lead you. When you own your choices and no longer make excuses or deflect accountability. When you find your fit, rather than hope things will work out on their own. When you think big(ger) instead of playing it safe. And finally, when you step off the sidelines and get in the game.

Even when you're fully in the game, there will always be ups and downs. Some days will be victorious, maybe even euphoric. Other days might feel like a gut punch. Don't be dismayed or deterred. Learn to find excitement in the tough stuff. Find strength in the pursuit and joy in the learning. Trust that the puzzle pieces of your life will come together. It won't happen overnight, but it will happen with intentional choices, consistent effort, and patience. The struggle or frustration that once overwhelmed you will dissipate. You'll get better at dealing with hard situations and won't be held back by them. You'll persevere.

When you need a boost or want to make a big play, return to this playbook. And know that we're your biggest superfans, quietly whispering in your ear and madly cheering you on. Because here's the simple truth: We believe in you. You can absolutely do this. Yes, you can. One hundred percent. Now you have the insight you need and the coaching guidance you've longed for.

And most of all, you have immense power within you to show up, level up, and move up. Use it!

Before you go

If something in these pages resonated with you—a story that felt familiar, a permission you needed to hear, a truth you'd been avoiding, we have one request.

Think of someone who could benefit from this book right now.

Maybe it's the woman in your office who's capable of so much more but can't see it yet. Maybe it's your friend who wants something bigger and better but doesn't know where to start. Or perhaps it's someone who's been waiting for a sign that it's okay to want something entirely different.

You know her. She probably came to mind just now.

Send her this book. Not because it has all the answers, but because sometimes we need someone else to say, "You're not imagining this" or "You're ready" or simply "Here's how."

And if you're willing, we'd love to hear *your* story. What happened after you closed this book? What did you learn about yourself? Where are you headed now? Share it with us at hello@equiptwomen.com. Or post your favorite tool or takeaway from the book on LinkedIn and Instagram along with the hashtags #UPbook and #EquiptWomen so we can repost your story on our pages.

Your journey might be exactly what inspires the next woman to take her first step.

Thank you for reading. Thank you for doing the work. And thank you for lifting *up* someone you care about.

Now go claim what's next for you.

Acknowledgments

Book covers are misleading—they feature only the authors' names when every book is truly a collective effort. This one required an entire community of friends, collaborators, challengers, and believers. While it's impossible to name everyone who contributed to this book, we extend our appreciation to all who offered their support, insights, and encouragement along the way. Any omissions are unintentional.

This book draws on decades of experience, including wild successes, massive failures, embarrassing missteps, and an earnest desire to keep learning and growing. As part of that journey, we're deeply grateful to the talented professionals we've worked with over the years. You've been our teachers, collaborators, and sometimes our mirrors. Many of the insights in this book were forged in the work we did together.

This book is also an extension of the work we've been doing since founding Equipt Women in 2021. The company was launched because we were (and still are) outraged by the fact that, despite women earning 59 percent of bachelor's degrees, they are paid and promoted at lower rates than men at every level. The issue starts with a woman's first job after college and persists throughout her career. We wanted to help more women develop the skills and confidence they needed to navigate a workplace that wasn't built by or for them. Equipt Women quickly gained momentum thanks to the support of those who believed in our mission to help women advance their careers and lead fulfilling lives. Thank you to Debbie Phillips, Diane Klein, Kate Delhagen, Troy Achong, and Kumi Walker for serving as Equipt Women's board of advisors, supporting its vision, and providing your seasoned insight. We salute the bold and trusting executive sponsors who partnered with Equipt Women, including J. P. Suarez, Emily Kokenge, Nathan Oliver, Bev Ryan, Sebastian Buck, Colleen Pero, Skyler Mattson, Bret Johnsen, Shannon Glass, Tara Agen, and Melissa Lemberg. These executives understand that organizations don't just survive—they thrive—when they invest in hiring, developing, and retaining diverse talent.

In the early days of creating Equipt Women programs, we tapped into the expertise of Candra Canning, Wilder Horng Brawer, Neelu Kaur, Noorin Fazal, Tiffany McDuffie, Hilary Davis, Joanna Miller, Jenny Sauer-Klein, Jeff Tritt, Darci Williams, Celine Krzan, and Amy Marzluff. Thank you for your insight, enthusiasm, and generosity.

We couldn't have done this without Karen Watts, our developmental editor. Thank you for helping us strengthen the outline, shape the structure of this book, and focus our message. Special recognition goes to Romi Benasuly, a rock star colleague who effortlessly wore many hats—researcher, fact-checker, sounding board, content contributor, project manager, and built-in target audience—with a smile and a can-do attitude. Thank you to Shelley Zalis, the founder and CEO of The Female Quotient, who shared her thoughtful words in the foreword, and for her pioneering entrepreneurship, dedicated to closing the global gender gap. A big hug goes to our talented friend and photographer, Tina Nieves, who captured the picture of us on the inside jacket, and to Andrea Cambern, who shared her stunning home for the photo shoot. We are grateful to Terry Rohrbach for designing the book cover that represents the positivity and power of our message.

We owe a debt of gratitude to Catherine Madrigal, Dilara Casey, Essence Spencer, Usheda Jackson, Riley Henningsen, Veronica Lopez, and Janine Gianfredi, who reviewed our original outline and provided us copious notes that improved our overall message. Dozens of people generously offered their insight and support along the way, including Andi Baldwin, Mike Bills, Jamie Barcelona, Angela Scott, Javier Feliciano, Tana Parrott, Malissia Clinton, Katherine von Jan, Kevin Rapp, Janet McCulley Kerslake, Ann Mooney, Amy Cooper, Dr. Jennifer Freed, Lisa Stein, and Megan Cunningham. The publishing industry is an especially difficult one to navigate, so we appreciate the guidance of Hali Lee, Gwyn Lurie, Clint Greenleaf, Rich Steel, Elise Loehnen, Ruth Milligan, and Doug Ulman.

To the team at Amplify Publishing, including Will Wolfslau, Jack Callahan, and Josh Taggert, thank you for your collaboration, expertise, and dedication to bringing this book to life. To the talented professionals at Smith Publicity, we are grateful for your creativity and commitment to helping this book find its readers.

A huge thank-you to the hundreds of women who participated in our programs and courageously shared your challenges, and to the tens of thousands of subscribers of the *Get Equipt* newsletter who continue to support our work and send us questions for future content. In addition, we extend our heartfelt appreciation to the 200 strangers from all over the world who responded to a LinkedIn post offering complimentary coaching in honor of International Women's Day. We hope you are proud to see your stories of openness, resilience, and determination reflected in these pages. You provided a front-row seat to the everyday struggles that women continue to face in today's workplace and beyond.

Last and most important to our partners in life, Scott Henningsen and Dean Backer, who love us unconditionally and enthusiastically support our tireless ambitions—and keep us well fed.

Bibliography

INTRODUCTION

top reason professional workers leave a job . . . : Parker, Kim, and Juliana Menasce Horowitz. "Majority of Workers Who Quit a Job in 2021 Cite Low Pay, No Opportunities for Advancement, Feeling Disrespected." Pew Research Center, March 9, 2022. https://www.pewresearch.org/short-reads/2022/03/09/majority-of-workers-who-quit-a-job-in-2021-cite-low-pay-no-opportunities-for-advancement-feeling-disrespected/.

momentum for advancing women in the workplace has stalled . . . : "Women in the Workplace." McKinsey & Company, 2024. https://www.mckinsey.com/featured-insights/diversity-and-inclusion/women-in-the-workplace.

Even though women are better educated . . . : "2025 Gender Pay Gap Report (GPGR)." Payscale Research, 2025. https://www.payscale.com/featured-content/gender-pay-gap.

PART 1

repeated behaviors strengthen neural pathways . . . : Wood, Wendy, and Dennis Rünger. "Psychology of Habit." *Annual Review of Psychology* 67 (January 4, 2016): 289–314. https://doi.org/10.1146/annurev-psych-122414-033417.

girls become more cautious . . . : Harris, Christine R., and Michael Jenkins. "Gender Differences in Risk Assessment: Why Do Women Take Fewer Risks Than Men?" *Judgment and Decision Making* 1, no. 1 (January 1, 2023): 48–63. https://doi.org/10.1017/S1930297500000346.

a strength is an activity that strengthens you . . . : Buckingham, Marcus. *StandOut 2.0.* Harvard Business Review Press, 2015.

how you feel before, during, and after an activity . . . : Adapted from Marcus Buckingham's SIGN tool. Buckingham, Marcus. *Go Put Your Strengths to Work.* Simon and Schuster, 2007.

just 17 percent say they employ their strengths . . . : Meier, J. D. "Spend 75 Percent on Your Strengths." Sourcesofinsight.com, 2023. https://sourcesofinsight.com/spend-75-percent-on-your-strengths/.

they're more engaged . . . : Seligman, Martin E. P., Tracy A. Steen, Nansook Park, and Christopher Peterson. "Positive Psychology Progress: Empirical Validation of Interventions." American Psychologist 60, no. 5 (2005): 410–21. https://doi.org/10.1037/0003-066x.60.5.410.

more creative . . . : Gallup. "The Innovation Equation." Gallup.com, April 12, 2007. https://news.gallup.com/businessjournal/27145/innovation-equation.aspx.

and happier: Seligman, Martin E. P., Tracy A. Steen, Nansook Park, and Christopher Peterson. "Positive Psychology Progress: Empirical Validation of Interventions." American Psychologist 60, no. 5 (2005): 410–21. https://doi.org/10.1037/0003-066x.60.5.410.

They learn faster, too: Brewerton, Dr. Paul. "What Is Strengths-Based Learning and Development and Why Does It Matter?" Strengthscope, February 28, 2022. https://www.strengthscope.com/blog/what-is-strengths-based-learning-and-development-and-why-it-matters.

clear understanding of what your strengths are!: I'm pumped/I'm drained adapted from Marcus Buckingham's Loved It/Loathed It tool. Buckingham, Marcus. *Go Put Your Strengths to Work*. Simon and Schuster, 2007.

80 percent of roles are filled as a result . . . : Ton, Jeffrey. "Council Post: Networking: It's Not What You Think." *Forbes*, August 12, 2024. https://www.forbes.com/councils/forbestechcouncil/2020/10/15/networking-its-not-what-you-think/.

70 percent or more of job opportunities . . . : Ton, Jeffrey. "Council Post: Networking: It's Not What You Think." *Forbes*, August 12, 2024. https://www.forbes.com/councils/forbestechcouncil/2020/10/15/networking-its-not-what-you-think/.

average annual income increase of 8.6 percent . . . : Gillespie, Lane. "Upskilling Statistics: How Online Learning Can Increase Your Salary by Thousands per Year." Yahoo Finance, March 27, 2023. https://finance.yahoo.com/news/upskilling-statistics-online-learning-increase-144832114.html.

39 percent of workers reported they advanced at their current job . . . : Gillespie, Lane. "Upskilling Statistics: How Online Learning Can Increase Your Salary by Thousands per Year." Yahoo Finance, March 27, 2023. https://finance.yahoo.com/news/upskilling-statistics-online-learning-increase-144832114.html.

certifications and licenses can boost weekly pay . . . : "Certifications Increase Annual Earnings | 2022 BLS Survey." ResumeBlaze, 2022. https://www.resumeblaze.com/increase-earnings-with-certifications.php.

PART 2

35,000 (mostly unconscious) decisions . . . : Reill, Amanda. "A Simple Way to Make Better Decisions." *Harvard Business Review*, December 5, 2023. https://hbr.org/2023/12/a-simple-way-to-make-better-decisions.

Circles of Influence framework . . . : Covey, Stephen R. *7 Habits of Highly Effective People*. New York: Simon & Schuster Ltd, 2020.

Adopt a mindset that helps you: Adapted from Carol Dweck's work on fixed mindset and growth mindset. Dweck, Carol S. *Mindset: The New Psychology of Success*. Random House, 2006. https://adrvantage.com/wp-content/uploads/2023/02/Mindset-The-New-Psychology-of-Success-Dweck.pdf.

only 52 percent of women feel comfortable . . . : Gupta, Shalene. "Why High-Earning Women Don't Want to Talk About Money." Fast Company, January 19, 2024. https://www.fastcompany.com/91012967/high-earning-women-finances-money-comfort.

Suze Orman has told people . . . : Trattner, Esther. "Suze Orman's 34 Biggest Money No-Nos." Moneywise, April 22, 2021. https://moneywise.com/a/ch-c/10-money-donts-from-suze-orman_SAFE-SuzeOJul3-WEFB-DSK/p-20?t=Suze%20Orman%E2%80%99s%2034%20Biggest%20Money%20No-Nos&hero=20200703112910040052675871.

PART 3

70 percent of employees say that when their work feels meaningful . . . : Dhingra, Naina, Andrew Samo, Bill Schaninger, and Matt Schrimper. "Help Your Employees Find Purpose—or Watch Them Leave." www.mckinsey.com, April 5, 2021. https://www.mckinsey.com/capabilities/people-and-organizational-performance/our-insights/help-your-employees-find-purpose-or-watch-them-leave.

44 percent of Gen Z and 45 percent of millennials . . . : "2025 Gen Z and Millennial Survey Growth and the Pursuit of Money, Meaning, and Well-Being." Deloitte, 2025. https://www.deloitte.com/content/dam/assets-shared/docs/campaigns/2025/2025-genz-millennial-survey.pdf.

32 percent of workers feel they're paid fairly . . . : "Gartner HR Research Finds Only 32% of Employees Believe Their Pay Is Fair." Gartner, November 28, 2022. https://www.gartner.com/en/newsroom/11-28-22-gartner-hr-research-finds-only-thirty-two-percent-of-employees-believe-their-pay-is-fair.

They are one of the top reasons . . . : Harter, Jim, and Marcus Buckingham. *First, Break All the Rules: What the World's Greatest Managers Do Differently.* New York: Gallup Press, 2016.

roughly 110,000 people quit their jobs daily . . . : "Job Openings and Labor Turnover Survey Home Page." US Bureau of Labor Statistics, July 19, 2008. https://www.bls.gov/jlt/.

6.6 employers from ages 25–52 . . . : "Baby Boomers Born from 1957 to 1964 Held an Average of 12.4 Jobs from Ages 18 to 54." US Bureau of Labor Statistics, September 3, 2021. https://www.bls.gov/opub/ted/2021/baby-boomers-born-from-1957-to-1964-held-an-average-of-12-4-jobs-from-ages-18-to-54.htm.

PART 4

"Why?" to understand the status quo . . . : "Five Whys for Inquiry." Clee.org, July 31, 2024. https://www.clee.org/resources/five-whys-for-inquiry/.

PART 5

people who regularly seek feedback . . . : Stone, Douglas, and Sheila Heen. *Thanks for the Feedback: The Science and Art of Receiving Feedback Well: (Even When It Is*

Off Base, Unfair, Poorly Delivered, and Frankly, You're Not in the Mood). London: Portfolio Penguin, 2014.

Gallup has long reported that having a best friend . . . : Patel, Alok, and Stephanie Plowman. "The Increasing Importance of a Best Friend at Work." Gallup.com, August 17, 2022. https://www.gallup.com/workplace/397058/increasing-importance-best-friend-work.aspx.

only 2 out of 10 people claim . . . : Patel, Alok, and Stephanie Plowman. "The Increasing Importance of a Best Friend at Work." Gallup.com, August 17, 2022. https://www.gallup.com/workplace/397058/increasing-importance-best-friend-work.aspx.

Yet, according to The Broken Rung . . . : Kweilin Ellingrud, Lareina Yee, and Maria del Mar Martinez. *The Broken Rung*. Harvard Business Press, 2025.

"nonpromotable work," meaning work that doesn't contribute . . . : Babcock, Linda, Brenda Peyser, Lise Vesterlund, and Laurie Weingart. *The No Club*. Simon and Schuster, 2022.

200 more hours annually on nonpromotable work . . . : Babcock, Linda, Brenda Peyser, Lise Vesterlund, and Laurie Weingart. "Are You Taking on Too Many Non-Promotable Tasks?" *Harvard Business Review*, April 26, 2022. https://hbr.org/2022/04/are-you-taking-on-too-many-non-promotable-tasks.

30 percent more likely than men . . . : LeanIn.org and McKinsey & Company. "Women in the Workplace 2024," 2016. https://womenintheworkplace.com/Women_in_the_Workplace_2016.pdf.

science shows it will make you happier . . . : Santi, Jenny. "The Secret to Happiness Is Helping Others." Time.com, 2017. https://time.com/collection/guide-to-happiness/4070299/secret-to-happiness/.

ADDITIONAL SOURCES

Cameron, Julia. *The Artist's Way: A Spiritual Path to Higher Creativity.* 1992. Reprint, S. L.: Profile Books Ltd, 2020.

Carroll, Anna. *The Feedback Imperative: How to Give Everyday Feedback to Speed Up Your Team's Success.* Austin, TX: River Grove Books, 2014.

Clear, James. *Atomic Habits: An Easy & Proven Way to Build Good Habits & Break Bad Ones.* New York: Penguin Publishing Group, 2018.

Flaherty, James. *Coaching: Evoking Excellence in Others.* London; New York: Routledge, Taylor & Francis Group, 2014.

Harter, Jim, and Marcus Buckingham. *First, Break All the Rules: What the World's Greatest Managers Do Differently.* New York: Gallup Press, 2016.

Rosenberg, Marshall B. *Nonviolent Communication: A Language of Life.* 3rd ed. Encinitas, CA: Puddledancer Press, 2015.

About the authors

Kelly Mooney founded Equipt Women to help aspiring women overcome systemic challenges and rise into roles of influence, leadership, and impact. She spent over two decades leading the nation's largest independent digital agency, guiding Fortune 500 clients through digital transformation. She has authored two additional books, created *Get Equipt*, a weekly email newsletter, and serves on the boards of public and private companies. She and her husband live in Santa Barbara, California, and have two thriving adult children and one spoiled Yorkie.

Katy Mooney is the cofounder and chief learning officer of Equipt Women. A performance coach and professional development expert, she's taught thousands of professionals at leading companies in Silicon Valley and beyond. Her career spans law, brand strategy, marketing leadership, entrepreneurship, and coaching—giving her a unique perspective on how to shape a career and life you love. She and her husband live in Santa Barbara, California, with their adorable dog, Sunny.

CONNECT WITH US

For more *UP!* resources, visit equiptwomen.com/upbook.

@pkmooney

@katymooney

@equipt-women

@equiptwomen

For weekly tips, tools, and strategies to advance your career and love your life along the way, **join Kelly's free weekly newsletter at equiptwomen.com/get-equipt.**